¡Viva Villa!

¡Hasta el último cartucho!

Pancho Villa
and
The End of Yankee Imperialism

Samuel Soto Ortega

Robert Baeza Hernandez

Errors and Omissions

The authors of **Viva Villa** have made a sincere effort to present the facts and circumstances regarding the Mexican Revolution to the best of their ability.

Many wonderful people have assisted with the editing, formatting, and have given direction on the preparation of **Viva Villa**. Nonetheless, any errors or omissions are the exclusive responsibility of the authors.

Contents

Contents

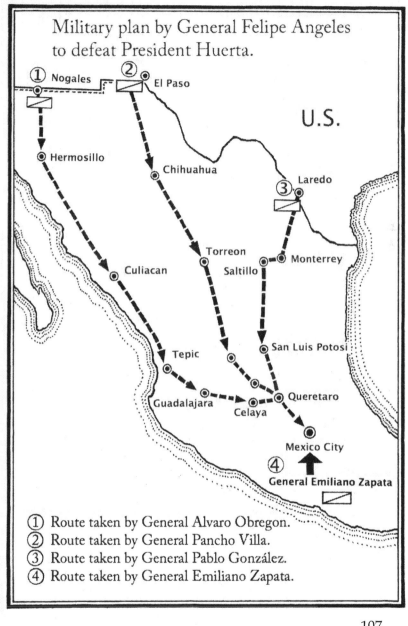

Military plan by General Felipe Angeles to defeat President Huerta.

① Route taken by General Alvaro Obregon.
② Route taken by General Pancho Villa.
③ Route taken by General Pablo González.
④ Route taken by General Emiliano Zapata.

Contents

Contents

Acknowledgments

In our home town of Sacramento, California, there is a sign on the local high school billboard that reads, "It takes a whole community to educate a child." Truer words have never been spoken when it comes to writing a book. This project could not have been possible without the assistance, guidance, and support of so many wonderful individuals. We are deeply indebted to all of them for the time they have so generously contributed.

There is no way to say thank you enough, but perhaps as they read the book, they will see how their edits and suggestions have given the book its final personality.

The authors wish to thank the following people for making *Viva Villa* possible:

Carlos Alcala, a legal expert, for his initial encouragement and guidance to prepare the book, and his contacts in El Paso, Texas. Louie Campos, MPH, for his effort to review the first draft of the manuscript, his constructive suggestions, and for making available his collection of books on the Revolution. Lucinda Chrisman, for her photography skills and camera work in developing photos to be included in the book. Tony Cervantes, Community Consultant, for his editing skills and suggestions for improving the final manuscript. John Castello, Esquire, recommendations on realigning certain chapters as well as his historical perspective. Walter Harmon of Camino, California, who allowed us to review his extensive library on the Mexican Revolution and for urging us to focus on the life of General Felipe Ángeles. Arnulfo Hernandez, Jr. Esquire for his editing skills and his compassion for keeping us focused in developing the thesis of the book. Manuel Hernandez, retired State of California legislative consultant, for his excellent editing skills and astute suggestions in clarifying certain historical issues. Elliot Loyd, California Department of Transportation (ret.), a good friend, and excellent reviewer of the first cumbersome drafts of the initial chapters. Adrian Lopez, the Dean of Yuba-Woodland Community Collage, for reading and re-editing the manuscript. Lupita Ochoa of Woodland, California, for her editing skills. Paul Ortega, Jr. for his research and initial draft regarding Villa's attack on Chihuahua, Chihuahua, Pedro Ramirez, professor at San Joaquin Delta Community College for his excellent editing skills and overall book assessment, Raymond Tafoya, California National Guard (ret.), for his reviews and edits. Xavier Tafoya, who contributed historical research and overall development of material for the book. Richard Soto, of Stockton, California, for making available his extensive collection of books on the Revolution.

Rene Quintanilla, Esquire, for his insightful review of the final manuscript, from a historical point of view, Gilbert Villareal Jr., for taking time to carefully edit several chapters, We also are indebted to Kenneth Umbach, as the initial editor of the manuscript before publication, especially his professional approach regarding the publication of a quality product, his diligence in editing the book, and his encouragement to remain patient during the hectic trials and tribulations of publishing a book.

We are indebted to Westley Turner who has been a partner from initial drafts to final publication. We could not have accomplished so much without his outstanding editing before final print and publication. His formatting of the book and his suggestions on organizing the material were of the utmost value, as well as his understanding and patience.

About the Book Cover

The book cover for Viva Villa was designed by Felipe Davalos, a world renowned illustrator whose works have been exhibited throughout the world.

Felipe was born in Mexico City, in what he likes to say, "A Family of Craftsmen." He learned his trade at an early age by working with his father who was master silversmith. He attended the Institute of Fine Arts in Mexico City, where he obtained a master's degree in copper, pottery, and textiles.

Felipe spent ten years fully immersed deep in the jungles of Mexico and South America where he became an expert on the origins and culture of the Aztec, Mayan, and Zapotec civilizations. He has transformed his knowledge and skill into masterpieces of art and illustration. He has been retained by the National Geographic Magazine and several American and European universities to reproduce master works of art. His most noteworthy work involved an assignment from National Geographic Magazine to produce an image of the Aztec Empire before the arrival of Hernan Cortes. For this assignment, he prepared a powerful and vibrant rendition of Tenochitlan, a city of over 200,000 inhabitants, and what is now Mexico City.

Felipe is a resident of Sacramento, California. He has written numerous books and travels throughout North America and Europe to make presentations on his extensive art collection.

According to Friedrich Katz

The Life and Times of Pancho Villa

Stanford University Press, 1998

"There is little doubt that new documents relating to and
new interpretations of both Villa and his movement
will emerge. In addition ... each generation will look at
Villa from a different perspective, so that discussions
on this subject will continue for a long time to come."

Preface

The Mexican Revolution lasted from 1910 to 1920. When it ended, it had cost more than one million willing and unwilling causalities, and most of the Revolutionary leaders had been assassinated. The Revolution was not an overnight plot by high-powered industrialists to take over the reins of government. It was a Revolution by the underdogs of the nation who were awakened to the realization that the regime of the Dictator President General Porfirio Diaz had to end. According to Niguel Hawthorne, "Tyrants, History's 100 Most Evil Despots & Dictators," Porfirio Diaz was ranked as the number 61 dictator of the century, in a list that includes Adolph Hitler and Benito Mussolini.

The seeds of the Revolution had been germinating for thirty years due to the economic policies of President Diaz and his concept of preferential treatment of foreign investors from the U.S. and European nations. Dictator Diaz had been in office over thirty years and ran the country with an iron fist. Anyone aspiring to be elected to a federal or state position could not do so without declaring his allegiance to the Diaz regime. He surrounded himself with a group of elderly cabinet members who called themselves Los Cientificos (generally meaning the learned ones). They believed they were blessed with superior knowledge and were the only ones who knew what was good for the nation because the peasants and campesinos who worked the lands were illiterate, unskilled, and too ignorant to choose their own leaders.

In the 1910 presidential elections, Francisco Madero successfully challenged the dictatorship of President Diaz. Madero ran on a platform to end the continuous reelection of Diaz to the Presidency. When it appeared that Madero would win the elections, President Diaz had him imprisoned until the elections were over. Madero escaped to San Antonio, Texas, where, on November 20, 1910, he issued the Plan de San Luis Potosi that called for a revolt against the Diaz dictatorship. (The Plan had been developed while he was in prison in the City of San Luis Potosi, State of San Luis Potosi, Mexico.) The boldness exhibited by President Diaz to deny Madero the Presidency set in motion five national conflicts of major proportions: the call by Madero, in 1910, for a national insurrection to remove Diaz from the Presidency; the rebellion, in 1911, by Emiliano Zapata for the return of ancestral lands; the revolt of General Pascual Orozco in 1911, against the Madero presidency; the "cuartelazo" (coup d'état), in 1913, by General Victoriano Huerta to steal the Presidency from Madero, and a preemptive strike in 1913, by General Venustiano Carranza to declare himself the "Primer Jefe" (First Chief) of the nation, for the purpose of removing General Huerta from a Presidency he had wrongfully assumed.

The decision by President Diaz to circumvent the election and deny Madero the Presidency sparked unrest in the nation for the next ten years. More importantly, the Diaz dynasty had not prepared the nation to deal effectively with an orderly transition of power in the event of presidential disruption. No one had anticipated that U.S. Ambassador Henry Lane Wilson would conspire with General Huerta to betray President Madero, or that Venustiano Carranza would arbitrarily install himself as the Primer Jefe of Mexico.

While President Diaz was in power, American and foreign investors earned enormous, tax free profits in mining operations, cattle ranches, oil exploration, manufacturing commerce and in the development of Mexico's railroad system. When Madero assumed the presidency, Mexico's relationship with foreign investors changed dramatically because they could no longer manipulate the presidency to their advantage. This change in the presidency did not sit well with the foreign investors and their political representatives, nor with their respective governments. The most overt actions against Madero were taken by U.S. Ambassador Henry Lane Wilson and General Victoriano Huerta.

Ambassador Wilson, who had been appointed by President Taft under the "Dollar Diplomacy" period, believed that Madero would take action to remove the preferential treatment accorded by President Diaz to American and foreign investors. The ambassador embarked on a program of defamation against Madero by informing President Taft that Madero was not fit to be President of Mexico. He sent untruthful communiqués stating that Madero did not have the support of the people of Mexico, and also began to openly consort with General Huerta and several others conspirators in secret to overthrow Madero.

On February 9, 1913, General Huerta, with the support of Ambassador Wilson, initiated a revolt against President Madero. Huerta ordered that President Madero and his Vice President José María Pino Suárez be arrested and sent to prison if they did not resign from office. When Madero and Pino Suárez refused to resign, Huerta had them imprisoned and later assassinated. As soon as Madero was eliminated, Huerta assumed the Presidency by pressuring the Mexican Congress to declare him the President of Mexico. The action taken by Huerta was contrary to the tenets of the Mexican Constitution, and soon, the Revolutionaries united to remove Huerta for having wrongfully assumed the presidency.

The betrayal of Huerta plunged the nation into an upheaval to determine who among the revolutionary leaders would be the true representative of Mexico. During this period of turmoil, the

U.S. exercised its military might by intervening in the internal affairs, as well as the occupation of Mexico, presumably to protect American lives, but most assuredly to protect American business investments, control the silver mines, and protect huge oil deposits. In 1913, after Huerta wrongfully assumed the presidency, President Wilson ordered a naval blockade of the Ports of Tampico and Veracruz to intimidate General Huerta into resigning his Presidency, and to stop the shipment of arms and munitions destined for General Huerta from Germany. The naval blockade, an act of war in violation of neutrality laws, involved the occupation of Veracruz by U.S. Marines for five months.

In October of 1915, President Wilson authorized the movement of the Mexican Army (Carranza troops) by railroad from Eagle Pass and Laredo, Texas to Douglas, Arizona, a distance of over 1,000 miles. The Mexican Army was transported on American railroads and American soil. As soon as the Mexican Army arrived at Douglas, Arizona, they walked across the border to fortify Agua Prieta, where Carranza troops inflicted a major military defeat against the forces of Pancho Villa.

Pancho Villa decided to retaliate against President Wilson for the action taken against him at Agua Prieta, and on March 7, 1916, Pancho Villa raided Columbus, New Mexico. Eighteen Americans and thirty Villistas were killed in the raid. On March 16, 1916, President Wilson ordered the deployment of 10,000 American cavalry troops, under the command of General John Pershing, to enter Mexico to capture Pancho Villa.

Fortunately for Mexico, Pancho Villa was able to avoid capture by staying one step ahead of General Pershing. Had General Pershing met his military objective of capturing Pancho Villa, Mexico would have been pressed to pay dearly for losing for a fourth time to the U.S. (the loss of Tejas in 1836, Texas

Annexation in 1845, and the War with Mexico of 1846-1848). With the presence of 10,000 U.S. cavalry troops deep in the interior of Mexico and the clamor by influential Americans, the authors believe that President Wilson would have acquiesced to the demands of expansionists and war mongers for the U.S. to acquire additional territory from Mexico. Had Pancho Villa been taken a prisoner of war, there is good reason to believe the U.S. would have taken possession of the border states of Sonora, Coahuila, Chihuahua, Nuevo Leon, and Tamaulipas, under the concept of "Protectorate Nation," a scheme employed by the United States in the past. Many would argue that the United States was not interested or capable of absorbing Mexican territory. This "holier than thou" point of view overlooks three earlier conflicts with Mexico: the Texas Revolt of 1836, when General Santa Anna was taken prisoner and forced to cede the territory of Tejas, the political campaign promise of President Polk for the annexation of Texas into the Union in 1845, and the loss of California and New Mexico Territories in the manufactured war of 1846-1848 with Mexico.

The failure of General Pershing to capture General Villa effectively brought an end to any further ambitions by the U.S. for westward expansion into Mexican territory, *planned or unplanned.* The fact that General Pancho Villa was not taken as a prisoner of war effectively prevented the U.S. from assuming control of Mexico's five border states.

Introduction

The purpose of this book is to acquaint the reader with the role played by Pancho Villa in the Mexican Revolution of 1910. The reader may want to refer to the books listed in the bibliography to gain other perspectives about the events of the Mexican Revolution.

We have focused on the key turning points of the Revolution: the conflict between Pancho Villa and Venustiano Carranza; the Convention of Aguascalientes; and the United States Punitive Expedition to capture Pancho Villa. The authors plan a sequel on the life and times of Emiliano Zapata, the other icon of the Mexican Revolution.

Over the years more than five hundred books have been written on the Mexican Revolution. On the American side, many of them have been written by scholarly professors from leading universities throughout the United States. These books present a treasure trove of knowledge which is necessary to understand why such a conflict could have lasted ten years (1910-1920) and cost the lives of one million people before the conflict ended. In spite of the many books written, there is, however, one serious consideration. Many of these books were written by Anglos whose culture and thinking emanate from an Americanized point of view.

This book is by Mexican-Americans who have enjoyed the benefits of a college education, have served in the administration of state government and the U.S. Military, and who also have cultural connections to the people of Mexico. The authors enjoy a bilingual and bi-cultural experience which is representative of some thirty-nine million Mexican-Americans who reside in the United States. This book is not a deep exercise in academics, for we do not claim to have taken three years of unending research to prepare the book, nor are we indebted to a certain university for research facilities or owe a great deal of gratitude to any particular foundation for financial support. This independence of thought has provided the authors with the essential latitude to focus on the relevant issues as viewed from a Mexican-American perspective. According to Fredrick Katz, one of the premier writers on the Mexican Revolution, "All generations have the right to recount history, particularly in view of the development of new historical information."

The genesis for the book started in 2008, while on a trip to Mexico, a trip that we have made many times. We had stopped for a few days to visit friends in San Antonio, Texas. The next leg of our journey would take us to the State of Chihuahua. After a few hundred miles into Mexico, we noticed a road sign that read City of Parral, Chihuahua, 45 kilometers (22 miles). We quickly realized this is the area where Pancho Villa fought many battles during the Revolution. This is also where he settled after he received amnesty and was given a hacienda by the government, after retiring from the Revolution; and where he was assassinated, in 1923.

Our inspiration to stop and visit was richly rewarded as we entered Parral and saw an awesome two-story bronze statue of Pancho Villa on horseback ready for the attack. A local docent with the Pancho Villa Museum in Parral shared with us a great deal of history about the Revolution. From that point on, as we travelled throughout the larger cities of Mexico, we gathered several books on the Revolution. From our college days and other general reading, we had some knowledge about the Revolution.

We were also privy to much of the folklore that had come out of the Revolution and shared with us by our parents, neighbors, and friends from Mexico. Many of our grandparents who came from the Mexico claimed they had left for the U.S. because they did not want to be conscripted to serve in the Revolution.

The more we read, the more we became enthused to learn more about the Revolution. As we devoured these books, it became apparent that Pancho Villa perhaps played the most dominant role during the ten years of the Revolution. From all the published material, we observed three dimensions about Pancho Villa. First, how could an undereducated and non-military person lead as many as 50,000 revolutionaries in battle after battle? Second, we were appalled at the extent of intervention by the conniving United States Ambassador Henry Lane Wilson in the internal affairs of Mexico. Third, we noted the nerve of President Woodrow Wilson to send General John Pershing with an invasion force into the interior of Mexico to capture Pancho Villa for the attack on Columbus, New Mexico, a small hamlet of minor military significance.

If a person asks the average reader about the pursuit of Pancho Villa by the U.S. Army, most would say that it was "justified" because Pancho Villa had "attacked American territory." If you ask a second question, "Are you aware of the international doctrine of Sovereign Rights and the laws of nations to enjoy a democracy?" one gets a look of being un-American. International borders are regarded as sacred by all nations of the world. Nations that subscribe to a legally constituted government have the right to enjoy their freedom and live in peace, without the fear of an invasion by a foreign army. When the U.S. entered Mexico, the expedition did not have the approval of Primer Jefe Venustiano Carranza, who made it clear that the U.S. was not welcome in Mexico.

Unfortunately, few people have accurate knowledge on the background and events that led Pancho Villa to attack Columbus. In the first part of the revolution (1910-1913), Pancho Villa was the darling of the American public and the American military. American film companies, newspapers and magazine journalists provided mass media coverage in recounting the great battles of the Revolution.

The noted author John Reed, on assignment from *Metropolitan* magazine, spent five months in the company of Villa covering the battles of the Villistas (the followers of General Pancho Villa), against the Federales (Federal Troops). From his experience with Villa, Reed wrote the book *Insurgent Mexico*, a day-to-day accounting of the determination and suffering of the underdogs who fought for the right to own a small plot of land that could provide a livelihood for their families. As long as Villa was winning battles, the U.S. military stationed along the Mexican border were delighted in taking photographs with Villa. On one occasion, General Hugh Scott, who became the Chief of Staff of the U.S. Army under President Wilson, offered Villa a pamphlet on the rules of war. On the American side, arms dealers with the full knowledge of the U.S. Government were more than eager to provide Villa, at a good profit, the rifles and bullets he needed to prosecute the Revolution.

When the Revolution started in 1910, the generals of the Revolution (Pascual Orozco, Pancho Villa, Emiliano Zapata, and Alvaro Obregón) all were united in one common effort to remove President Porfirio Diaz. However, fifteen months after Francisco Madero assumed the Presidency, General Victoriano Huerta and U.S. Ambassador Henry Lane Wilson conspired to have President Madero and Vice President Pino Suárez removed, and later assassinated. Once again these generals were united, this time to remove General Huerta for having wrongfully assumed the Presidency. General Huerta served only seventeen months before he was exiled to live in Spain.

However, during the process to remove General Huerta, Villa and Carranza became bitter enemies. Villa believed that Carranza would become another dictator just like Diaz, who would not act in the best interest of Mexico. To settle the question of leadership between Villa and Carranza, in 1914 the Revolutionary leaders convened the Convention of Aguascalientes to determine who should be the true leader of Mexico. They were not able to resolve their differences and, in the end, they separated into two armed camps, the Constitutionalists for Carranza and Obregón, and the Conventionists for Villa and Zapata.

After many battles between the forces of Villa and Carranza, the U.S. aligned itself with the forces of Carranza. The turning point for Villa was the defeat of his army by General Alvaro Obregón in the two major battles in the City of Celaya in the State of Guanajuato. In the first battle, on April 7, 1915, Villa lost some 5,000 troops. One week later, on April 16, he attacked Celaya again and this time he lost another 3,000 troops. From this point on, Villa's fortunes began to decline and he would no longer be able to command the large armies that had brought him victories against Diaz, Orozco, and Huerta.

After the devastating loss at the City of Celaya, Villa needed to rebuild his army and decided to attack the City of Agua Prieta, situated across from the border town of Douglas, Arizona. At Agua Prieta, Villa could take possession of the customs house and its revenue, as well as take horses and munitions. When Villa planned his attack, he expected to face some 1,500 Carranza troops commanded by General Plutarco Calles. However, unbeknown to Villa, President Wilson had authorized the U.S. Army to transport to the scene of battle an additional 5,000 Carranza troops. Due to this action by the U.S. Army when Villa carried out his attack on Agua Prieta, he faced 6,500 Carranza troops instead of the 1,500 he expected. Villa suffered another major defeat and had to retreat to more familiar ground to regroup in the State of Chihuahua.

Villa was convinced he was defeated at Agua Prieta because of the military support provided to Carranza by President Wilson. In retaliation for the betrayal by President Wilson, Villa decided to attack Columbus, New Mexico. The attack occurred on March 9, 1916, and within one week of the attack the U.S. deployed a large invasion force to march into the interior of Mexico for the single purpose of capturing Villa. Since the military reaction was so swift and powerful, it is reasonable to conclude that the U.S. Army had for some time been making war plans to occupy Mexico.

The available historical evidence does not indicate the U.S. made an effort to discuss with Carranza how Villa should be brought to justice for violating the laws of the U.S. Fortunately for Mexico, the failure of General Pershing to capture Villa exposed the military might and arrogant intent of the U.S. to teach Mexico a lesson, an arrogance that was all too familiar in past relationships between the two countries.

The ability of Villa to outlive his adversaries, to command of up to 50,000 troops and his reputation as a Robin Hood who would take from the rich to give to the poor, and his ability to evade capture by General Pershing have endeared Villa to many people in Mexico and throughout the world. The amount of literature dedicated to his endeavors, the folklore of those who fought with him, his distaste for the well-to-do and the many monuments dedicated to him in cities throughout Mexico, including his place of honor in the National Memorial to the Revolution in Mexico City, have transformed Villa into an icon known all over the world. It has been often said that Villa was "hated by a thousand people, but he was loved by millions." He is especially revered by the people of Mexico. Once introduced to the Revolution, he fought for the underdog with ferocity and determination, as only a few others did.

Part One – European and United States Dominance

For almost five hundred years, Mexico has been invaded by Spain, France, and the United States. The most enduring of these intrusions was the invasion and conquest of the Mexica Empire by Spain. The Spaniards dominated Mexico from 1521 to 1821, a period of three hundred years. When the Spaniards arrived, Mesoamerica had a population of over twenty million inhabitants. By waging war against the inhabitants, using them as slave labor during empire building, and introducing European diseases, the Spanish reduced the indigenous population to five million people. They plundered the vast resources of the nation by sending gold and silver to Spain, imposed the Spanish language, and introduced Catholicism as the state religion. They introduced the devastating notion of vast land grants named Encomiendas (large feudal estates awarded to elite Spaniards that required the native people to work as slaves in order to generate profits).

Although Mexico gained its independence in 1821, Mexico continued to be subjected to intervention, invasion, and occupation by Spain, France, and the United States. The first attempt occurred in 1829, when Spain attempted to re-conquer Mexico. This was followed by the revolt of the Anglo-Texans in 1836 to become an independent state, the U.S. Annexation of Texas in 1845 that led to war with Mexico, the War with Mexico in 1846 regarding the international boundary between the United States and Mexico, the occupation of Mexico by the French in 1861 to collect a national debt, the naval blockade of the Port of Tampico, the occupation of the Port of Veracruz in 1914 by the United States to stop arms and munitions from reaching the

1

regime of General Victoriano Huerta, and the invasion of General Pershing in 1916 into the interior of Mexico to capture Pancho Villa for having attacked Columbus, New Mexico.

The extent of invasion, occupation, and intervention in Mexico by the U.S. has been well documented by many historians. In a book authored by noted military historian Brigadier General John D. Eisenhower (son of former U.S. President and WW II Supreme Allied Commander Dwight Eisenhower), "The War between the United State and Mexico, 1846-48", Eisenhower adopted the theme of "Poor Mexico, so far from God and so Close to the United States". The implication was that Mexico had a twofold problem: the Catholic Church would constantly dominate the religious development of Mexico's indigenous people, and Mexico would also be constantly subject to the territorial ambitions and the military might of the United States.

Historical Chronology

1521	The Conquest of the Mexica Empire
1821	End of Spanish Rule Period
1823	American Settlement in Tejas
1829	Effort by Spain to Re-conquer Mexico
1836	The Texas Revolt
1838	The French Occupation of Veracruz
1845	The Annexation of Texas
1846	United States War with Mexico
1853	The Republic of Baja California
1861	The Imperialism of France
1914	United States Intervention at Tampico
1914	United States Naval Blockade of Veracruz
1915	United States Intervention at Agua Prieta
1916	United States Occupation of the State of Chihuahua
1919	Intervention at Ciudad Juarez

International Agreements

1853	The Sale of La Mesilla (The Gadsden Purchase)
1977	United States/Mexico Agreement on El Chamizal

Invasion and Conquest of the Mexica Empire

In 1519, Hernan Cortes sailed from Cuba to land near Veracruz with 600 soldiers to capture the City of Tenochtitlan (what is now Mexico City), a thriving commercial center with over 200,000 inhabitants. (See map for route taken by Cortes, and photo of City of Tenochtitlan, at end of chapter.) There are several reasons why Cortes was able to conquer the Mexicas. According to some historians, the most important reasons include: the services of Dona Marina, an important ally for Cortes who could speak the Nahuatl language; the strategy by Cortes to develop an alliance with the Tlaxcalan Indians; and the fact that his army was equipped with horses, armor, and muskets, things unknown to the Mexicas.

Cortes initially landed in the area of Yucatan, but there he found the Mayans to be fierce warriors, so he decided to explore further north. From the skirmishes with the Mayans, Cortes was given a Mexica slave woman by the name of Dona Marina, who had been captured by the Mayans. Because she could speak the Mayan and Nahuatl languages, she played a crucial role in the defeat of the Mexicas. In Mexico, Dona Marina is often referred to as "La Malinche" a derogatory term that came to imply treason or back stabbing. When Cortes landed near Veracruz, Dona Marina served him well by communicating with the Totonac Indians, who hated the Mexicas because of their belief in offering their enemy as human sacrifice.

Through Dona Marina, Cortes also established an alliance with the Tlaxcala Indians, who agreed to join the army of Cortes and provide him with 100,000 warriors. They served as scouts and were willing to carry munitions and supplies over the

4

mountainous area of Veracruz and Puebla to reach the beautiful, and highly developed, City of Tenochtitlan, the capital of the Mexica Empire.

When Cortes arrived in Mexico, his army numbered some 600 Spanish soldiers compared to some 100,000 Mexica warriors. Since Emperor Moctezuma had superior numbers, he could have easily defeated Cortes, except that Cortes had a modern army, was able to develop an alliance with the Tlaxcalan Indians, and the Mexicas were superstitious. From the moment that Cortes landed in Veracruz, his progress towards Tenochtitlan was tracked by the scouts of Emperor Moctezuma. He even tried to appease Cortes by sending him elaborate gifts made of gold, but this only served to further whet Cortes's appetite to seek golden treasures to be sent to the King of Spain. Moctezuma learned too late that Cortes only wanted gold, and for this failure he was stoned to death by his own people.

After the death of Moctezuma, his nephew, Cuauhtemoc, became the emperor. Cuauhtemoc was very brave, and he refused to tell Cortes where the Mexica gold and treasures were hidden. To find the hidden gold, the Spaniards tortured Cuauhtemoc by burning his feet, but Cuauhtemoc would rather suffer death for his people than to surrender. For his act of bravery, many families in Mexico have named their sons Cuauhtemoc, as in the case of Cuauhtemoc Cardenas, Mayor of Mexico City and one time candidate for President of Mexico.

Spanish Rule and the Colonial Period

After the defeat of the Mexica Empire, Mexico was governed by successive Viceroys appointed by the King of Spain, whose main interest was to harvest all of the riches of Mexico to support the

King of Spain and also underwrite other expeditions. At first, the Spaniards were destroying the native population with brutality and European diseases such as smallpox and the bubonic plague. Later they recognized they needed the native population to perform the necessary labor to work the mines, build roads and buildings, and build the Catholic Missions along the El Camino Real. The Indians worked like slaves, performing hard labor. They had no rights to own land, vote, or move about the country. The Spanish had no interest in developing a democracy, in contrast to the events taking place in the thirteen British colonies of North America.

Spain had no desire to establish a democratic form of government to prepare the citizenry to assume the reins of government at some time in the future. In 1821, it is estimated that Mexico was controlled by some 15,000 Gachupines (persons born in Spain) and over one million Creoles (full blood Spaniards who were born in Mexico). In this manner, the Spaniards controlled all commercial trade, government, church, wine and textile industries, as well as the military. Thus, when Mexico revolted against Spain, there were few Mestizos (persons of mixed blood between Spaniards and the native population) with any practical experience in the administration of government, and in effect, the new citizens were not prepared to govern the internal affairs of an emerging nation.

On September 15, 1810, a rebellious priest in the State of Guanajuato, Miguel Hidalgo y Costilla, seized a flag with the embodiment of Our Lady of Guadalupe and declared that the people of Mexico would no longer be the subjects of the King of Spain. The outcry by Priest Hidalgo for freedom from the Spanish yoke did not last very long. Father Hidalgo and three of his co-conspirators were captured March 21, 1811. Father Hidalgo and his followers were executed by the Spanish Army on July 30, 1811, in the City of Guanajuato. Their decapitated heads were placed on each of the four corners of the two story grain storage warehouse (bodega) in the City of Guanajuato for the populace to see that Spain was not going to tolerate independence. After the initial declaration of independence there were many battles against the Spaniards until 1821, when under the Treaty of Cordova, Spain agreed that Mexico was a separate and independent nation.

After independence, with the exception of the Presidency of Benito Juarez, Mexico was governed for almost 87 years by a number of dictators whose main interest was to stay in office in perpetuity. Mexico had few examples of progressive and democratic statesmanship. This was evident from the beginning when Agustin Iturbide, who was selected as the first leader of the nation, named himself as the Emperor of Mexico. This was clear indication that the nation had not moved away from a monarchy and the title-oriented Spanish form of government. Moreover, although Mexico had gained independence, the nation's infrastructure was dominated by the Spaniards who had stayed in Mexico and continued to control the banks, haciendas, mines, and government offices (both state and federal).

American Settlement in Tejas in 1823

In 1820, Moses Austin, an empresario from the State of Louisiana, petitioned Antonio Maria Martinez, the Governor of the Coahuila-Tejas Territory, for a settlement of 300 American families in the territory of Tejas. Governor Martinez granted the request in 1821 because the Tejas territory was geographically isolated from Mexico City and at such a distance there was a need for the territory to be populated to discourage encroachment by other foreign nations. More importantly, Mexico was concerned it did not have the military might to protect its northernmost territory.

As condition for settling in Tejas, the Americans, led by Stephen Austin (the son of Moses Austin) agreed to obey the laws of Mexico, develop the land agriculturally, pay taxes, and adopt Catholicism. In return, Mexico agreed it would not collect taxes for the first fifteen years. When the Americans settled in Tejas, they were considered part of the Coahuila territory, that are now the states of Coahuila and Texas (the seat of government was in Coahuila). Soon more Anglos than had been agreed to started to arrive, and the Mexican Government was forced to declare Tejas to be off limits for Anglo Texans.

From the beginning, it became clear that the Anglo Texans had no intention of conforming to the laws of Mexico. Due to language differences and lack of political representation from Coahuila, the Americans declared the Mexican laws to be intolerable. In reality, due to language and cultural differences from Mexico and homogeneity with the U.S. population, the Anglo Texans felt they owed their allegiance to the U.S. In addition, the majority of the Anglo Americans that settled in Tejas were proslavery, yet slavery was illegal according to the Mexican Constitution (during the Civil War of 1860, Texas was one of the states to secede from the Union in support of slavery).

Based on so-called "intolerable acts" on the part of the Mexican Government, in 1836, the Anglo-Texans revolted to gain their independence. (It should be noted that the Americans declared the laws of Mexico as "intolerable" after only thirteen years of living as guest immigrants.) To end the Anglo revolt, General Santa Anna mobilized 5,000 troops and marched to San Antonio, Texas, to engage the Americans in the Battle of the Alamo.

Although heavily outnumbered, the Americans and some Mexican-Texans who also wanted independence defended the Alamo for thirteen days until all 150 defenders were killed or wounded. Despite the setback at the Alamo, final victory came to the Americans on April 21, 1836, when General Sam Houston defeated Santa Anna at the Battle of San Jacinto. After the loss at San Jacinto, Santa Anna agreed to cede Tejas to the new republic. (The Treaty of Velasco, which was never ratified by the Mexican Congress because it was signed under duress.) Eventually, Tejas became The Republic of Texas, with its own flag, and Sam Houston became its first president. Although Santa Anna had signed the agreement, he was nonetheless kept prisoner by the U.S. for several months.

The Invasion by Spain in 1829

After Mexico became an independent nation, there remained in Mexico thousands of Spaniards who yearned to return to the days of Spanish Rule. In 1829, they made plans to retake Mexico. The invasion was conceived in Cuba by General Dionisio Vives, the military commander for Cuba. The invaders assumed they would be welcomed in Mexico because of dissatisfaction and unrest. They believed that once they landed in Mexico, they would be received with open arms and be provided horses, munitions, and military support. However, the information they received was incorrect because the dissatisfaction they perceived did not exist.

The Spanish invasion of 1829 was led by General Isidro Barradas. His 3,500 troops included 3,000 soldiers, 300 cavalry, and 200 artillerymen. On August 15, 1829, General Barradas landed at the Port of Tampico in the State of Tamaulipas. His troops moved immediately inland expecting minimal resistance.

The Spaniards were wrong in their assessment regarding armed resistance. Through diplomatic channels and other intelligence sources, Mexico had learned of the departure of the invasion force from Havana, Cuba, and was well aware of the invasion date. With this advance knowledge, Mexico was able to mobilize an army under General Mier y Teran, who later transferred his authority to General José Antonio Lopez de Santa Anna, as the Commander of all Defensive Forces. The Spanish penetrated as far as the City of Tampico, where a number of skirmishes took place near the River Panuco. The Spaniards soon realized that they had an inferior number of soldiers, they did not have local partisan support, and the Mexican Army had deployed more rapidly than they had expected.

In view of the odds against them, the Spaniards initiated several peace talks and eventually agreed to surrender and leave Mexico. Having been decisively defeated, the Spaniards surrendered on September 11, 1829, and were allowed safe passage to return to Havana, Cuba. Of the 3,500 Spanish troops that invaded Mexico, only 1,792 returned. The other 1,708 were either war causalities or died of tropical disease.

French Occupation of Veracruz in 1838

In 1838, the French sent a naval armada to block the Port of Veracruz to collect monies from Mexico. During its struggle for independence in 1821, Mexico had borrowed monies from France and for several years Mexico was unable to repay its debt. In 1838, street fighting took place to determine who would stay in power in Mexico. During this period of turmoil, French citizens incurred damage to their businesses and property. One French citizen in particular, Monsieur Remontel claimed damages to his bakery business. Remontel and other French citizens asked the French

Government to intervene to collect for the damages inflicted, or about 600,000 pesos. Mexico was unable to pay the debt and the French Government ordered the occupation of Veracruz.

Since Mexico did not have a large navy to defend itself, the French were able to occupy Veracruz. As a settlement, Mexico agreed to pay the 600,000 pesos and the French Fleet returned to France in March of 1839. Some historians refer to this episode as the "French Pastry War."

Annexation of Texas in 1845

In 1845, after nine years as an independent nation, The Republic of Texas petitioned the U.S. for annexation. Initially, the true desire of the power brokers who initiated the Texas revolt of 1836 was for Texas to become a new empire by acquiring the territories of California, Arizona, and New Mexico. They envisioned a new empire that spanned from Galveston, Texas on the Gulf of Mexico to Monterey, California on the Pacific Ocean. However, the visionaries were not able to gain the necessary support and instead they settled for annexation by the U.S. The annexation was opposed by Mexico for two principal reasons. Mexico was quite sure that annexation would lead to war with the U.S. over a proper and correct boundary line between the two nations, and Mexico was convinced that the overt activity for annexation was a clear signal that the U.S. wished to continue its policy of westward expansion.

Mexico made many objections against annexation and vehemently informed the U.S. that annexation would eventually lead to war between the two nations. In spite of these protests, on December 29, 1845, Congress voted for the annexation of Texas into the Union. Annexation was a foregone conclusion, considering that the political plank for the presidency of James Polk in 1844 included the annexation of Texas. Once James Polk was elected, he moved quickly to execute his political agenda to annex Texas regardless of any U.S. Congressional opposition.

United States War with Mexico in 1846

After Texas joined the Union, the U.S. continued with its westward expansion doctrine. Before the start of war with Mexico, the United States made an offer to purchase California for forty million dollars and a separate offer to purchase Baja California. Mexico rejected both offers to sell its territory. This only served to inflame the ambition of the U.S. to possess California, by force if necessary. The United States wanted California desperately because, since the days of the Californios, it was known that California was a large and rich territory. The Americans were aware that the port of Monterey had become a hub of international trade where foreign ships paid a duty to unload their commodities. The ships would arrive with European goods and leave with olive oil, tomatoes, fruit, and animal skins. In addition, the U.S. was concerned that if California was not occupied and fortified, perhaps it might fall into the hands of another European seafaring nation, such as France or England.

To start the war, the U.S. manufactured the question as to the proper line of demarcation between the two countries, just as Mexico had predicted. The United States set the boundary at the Rio Grande River while Mexico maintained the line was at the Nueces River. To reaffirm its position, the United States sent an army detachment to occupy a small strip of land near the Rio Grande River. The Army built a military post (what is now Brownsville, Texas), raised the American flag, and served notice to Mexico that the disputed parcel belonged to the U.S. Mexico notified the U.S. that if the army outpost was not removed, there would be war between the two nations. The U.S. ignored the warnings and on April 25, 1846, Mexico acted to remove the army outpost. Sixteen Americans and an unknown number of Mexicans were killed in the initial skirmish. President Polk, who authorized the confrontation, had counted on the fact that Mexico would act to defend its territorial rights. As soon as President Polk was informed of the skirmish, he asked Congress to declare war with Mexico because Americans had been killed and American blood had been spilled defending the honor of the U.S. The U.S. did not request an investigation regarding the skirmish at the border. The U.S. simply blamed Mexico, and war with Mexico was declared by Congress on May 15, 1846.

Mexico was no match for the military might of the U.S. In nine months the U.S. Army travelled by land to occupy all of Northern Mexico and on March 9, 1847, it landed a naval force in Veracruz that marched inland to occupy Mexico City. Having been defeated, Mexico signed the Treaty of Guadalupe Hidalgo whereby it surrendered the territories of California, Arizona, Nevada, New Mexico, and parts of the states of Wyoming, Colorado, and Utah. By this action, Mexico surrendered almost one half of the land mass that it had acquired only 35 years earlier from Spain. It is interesting to note that neither the U.S. nor any neutral nation offered to enter into negotiations for a reasonable settlement regarding the disputed boundary line regarding the Nueces River. In effect, there were no negotiations. The U.S., being the superior power, simply dictated to Mexico that it give up almost one half of its territory, or risk losing all of it. The amount of land acquired by the U.S. was overwhelmingly disproportionate in relation to the original dispute. Mexico claimed the Nueces River and the U.S. claimed the Rio Grande River as the boundary line. Assuming that the U.S. claim was correct, the two countries should have concluded a settlement establishing the Rio Grande as the permanent boundary line. No explanation has been offered as to why the U.S. gained control and ownership over the California, Arizona, and New Mexico territories. Occupation of the California, Arizona, and New Mexico territories were not the stated reason that the U.S. declared war against Mexico.

The William Walker Occupation of Baja California

William Walker graduated from the University of Tennessee at age 14 and travelled throughout Europe as a young man. At age 19 he received a medical degree from the University of Pennsylvania. He also studied and practiced law in New Orleans. Walker moved to San Francisco, California, where he worked as a journalist. On October 15, 1853, Walker set out with 45 men to conquer Baja California and the State of Sonora. His expedition was financed by several wealthy entrepreneurs from San Francisco. His intention was to set up the Independent Republic of Sonora along the lines of the Independent Republic of Texas of 1836. Walker landed in La Paz, Baja California, where he declared himself the President of Baja California, and adopted laws to make slavery legal. When his munitions ran low and he met resistance from the Mexican Government, he returned to the U.S. Walker was put on trial for conducting an illegal war in violation of the Neutrality Act of 1794. Although he had violated the Neutrality Act, Walker had gained a great deal of support from expansionists for his daring to conquer Baja California, and he was eventually acquitted.

Walker was not discouraged from becoming an expansionist. In 1855, Walker obtained permission from President Castellon of Nicaragua to bring 300 colonists to Nicaragua. When Walker landed, he had the support of 160 Americans and 170 Nicaraguans. On October 13, 1855, Walker took control of Nicaragua and was named commander of all military forces. He ruled Nicaragua through the puppet government of President Patricio Rivas. On May 20, 1856, U.S. President Franklin Pierce recognized Walker's regime as the legitimate government of Nicaragua.

By 1857, Walker lost his foothold in Nicaragua and was repatriated to the U.S. In 1860, he tried to occupy Honduras, but was captured and placed before a firing squad. He was 36 years old when he was executed.

The Imperialism of France in 1861

In 1861, France declared that Mexico had not paid the monies it had borrowed to gain its independence from Spain. In retribution for nonpayment, France invaded Mexico and proceeded to establish a new monarchy by installing the Archduke Maximilian of Hapsburg, Austria, as the Emperor of Mexico. On May 5, 1862, underrated Mexican troops defeated some 5,000 French invaders in the City of Puebla, located about 80 miles from Mexico City. Hence the Cinco de Mayo is celebrated annually by Mexican-Americans throughout United States. The French regrouped and returned with 15,000 invaders to occupy Mexico City. The French occupation and the notion of French monarchy were never accepted in Mexico. The Archduke and his wife Carlotta were childless, and towards the end of his Monarchy, the Archduke

15

made an effort to appease the Mexican populace by presenting the six-year-old grandson of Mexico's Emperor Agustin Iturbide as the future Monarch of Mexico.

The effort to appease the nation was rejected by the Mexican people for the façade that it was. President Benito Juarez, a native Indian from the State of Oaxaca, rose to the occasion as an astute statesman. He was able to lead an insurrection that forced the French Army to leave Mexico. Without the presence of the French Army, the Archduke was obliged to surrender his monarchy to the army of Benito Juarez. In spite of many pleas for his life by several nations, on June 19, 1867, the Archduke Maximilian and his Mexican supporters were executed in the City of Queretaro, in the State of Guanajuato. It was the intent of Benito Juarez to send a message to other nations that foreign occupation of Mexico carried a high price.

U.S. Intervention in the Mexican Revolution of 1910

President Wilson was offended by the manner in which General Huerta had assumed the Presidency and vowed to have him removed, by force if necessary. To ensure the downfall of General Huerta and to prevent munitions from reaching him from Europe, President Wilson ordered the U.S. Navy to blockade the Ports of Tampico and Veracruz. On April 21, 1914, the United States landed 3,500 marines and sailors at the Port of Veracruz, and occupied Veracruz for six months.

The Pursuit of Pancho Villa by General Pershing

On March 9, 1916, in retaliation for the military support provided by President Wilson to Primer Jefe Carranza at Agua Prieta,

Pancho Villa invaded the small hamlet of Columbus, New Mexico to seize arms, horses, and food supplies.

Ten citizens and eight soldiers were killed by the Villistas. In retribution, President Wilson ordered the American Army to enter the interior of Mexico to capture Pancho Villa. General John Pershing pursued Villa in the mountains of Chihuahua and Durango for twelve months without ever engaging the guerrilla fighter. During the Villa campaign, the U.S. lost 27 and Villa lost 250 soldiers. More importantly, the military losses by Pershing were sustained by fighting against the forces of Venustiano Carranza, not the army Pancho Villa. The disastrous campaign of General Pershing lasted one year. It ended in February 1917, when Pershing and his army reentered the U.S. at El Paso, Texas.

International Agreements with the United States

Two other international issues affected relations between the U.S. and Mexico: the Gadsden Purchase and El Chamizal. These two issues did not involve a military invasion or occupation. They are noted by the authors because many people assume the Gadsden Purchase and El Chamizal involved military action or were part of the fighting involved in the Revolution, which was not the case.

The Gadsden Purchase

The Gadsden Purchase was completed in 1853, when an area known as La Mesilla was purchased by the U.S. for $10 million. La Mesilla is a tract of land along the border between the states of Arizona and Sonora. The U.S. wanted the land to build a railroad with access to New Mexico and Texas. In the end the railroad was not built at La Mesilla, but instead it was built to go through Las Cruces, New Mexico. The Gadsden Purchase is named after James Gadsden who was the Secretary of State under President Franklin Pierce.

Agreement on El Chamizal

El Chamizal is a small tract of waterway between the United States (El Paso) and Mexico (Ciudad Juarez). Over the years, the boundary between the two cites changed due to the flow of the Rio Grande River. Over time, a new land mass of 559 acres was created. In 1963, a settlement was arrived at whereby new land mass was divided between the two countries. The U.S. gained 193 acres, and Mexico gained 366 acres. The countries also agreed to build a cement retainer to prevent further land movement. The settlement was signed by President Lyndon Johnson on January 14, 1963. While no money was paid by either country to the other for the exchange in land, the U.S. received compensation from Mexico for several buildings that it lost when land was exchanged between the two countries.

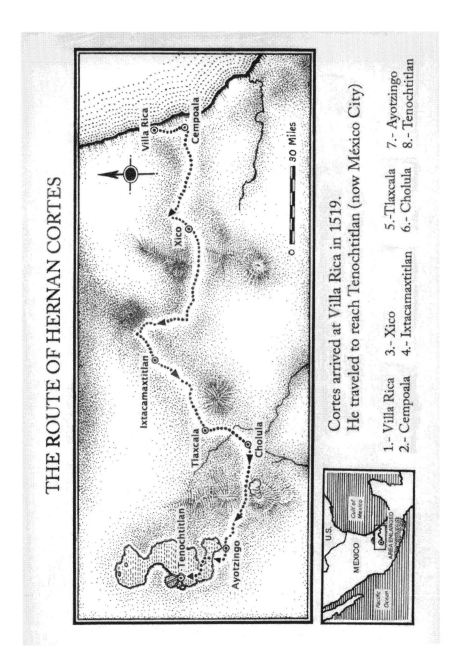

THE ROUTE OF HERNAN CORTES

Cortes arrived at Villa Rica in 1519.
He traveled to reach Tenochtitlan (now México City)

1.- Villa Rica	3.- Xico	5.-Tlaxcala	7.- Ayotzingo
2.- Cempoala	4.- Ixtacamaxtitlan	6.- Cholula	8.- Tenochtitlan

When the Spaniards arrived at Tenochitlan (now Mexico City) they could not believe they were seeing a city of over 200,000 inhabitants. The city included merchants, tax collectors, and four causeways for access to the city. The Spaniards had not seen a city as large or as beautiful in all of Spain.

Part Two – The Mexican Revolution of 1910

Chapter I.   Doroteo Arango Becomes Pancho Villa

At age sixteen, Doroteo Arango became a fugitive. He spent the next sixteen years in the hills of Durango and Chihuahua as a bandolero. He was almost captured nine times and on one occasion was wounded in the chest. While on the run, Doroteo learned to survive by cunning and warrior instincts. He valued loyalty above all else and wrought heavy-handed retribution on those who betrayed him. Doroteo tried to become an ordinary citizen, but each time he tried he was betrayed by persons who knew there was a price on his head. (See map #2 at end of chapter for Doroteo Arango hiding places.)

Doroteo was born on June 5, 1878, at the Hacienda Rio Grande in the State of Durango. His birthplace is near the village of San Juan del Rio near the municipality of Parral, Chihuahua (Parral is next to the State of Durango). His parents, Agustin Arango and Micaela Arambula, were sharecroppers on the hacienda owned by Agustin Lopez Negrete. Doroteo was the oldest of five children, brothers Hipolito, Antonio, and sisters Maríana and Martinita. When his father died, he became the head of the family at age fifteen. He continued working as a ranch hand and sharecropper for Don Agustin Lopez Negrete at the Hacienda "El Gogojito" where he learned to handle horses with great ability. Doroteo eventually became an expert horseman and a sharpshooter.

At age sixteen, as he returned home from his ranching chores, he came upon his mother who was confronting the son of the hacendado Lopez Negrete for having accosted Martinita, age fourteen. The mother was imploring the son of Lopez Negrete to leave Martinita alone. Upon seeing the abuse being perpetrated by the hacendado, Doroteo became incensed and immediately went to the home of his cousin, Romauldo Franco, where he kept a revolver handy. Armed with a loaded pistol he went looking for Lopez Negrete and when he found him he fired several rounds, wounding him in the leg. Five of the hacendado's workers retrieved their rifles to arrest Doroteo, but Lopez Negrete insisted that instead, he be returned to the Hacienda San Isabel de Berros for medical attention. At that moment Doroteo knew he had to escape because he would surely be incarcerated.

In those primitive days justice was swift against the campesinos because the landowners were protected by the dictator, President Diaz, who controlled the countryside with his infamous Rurales (comparable to the Texas Rangers). When someone escaped, the Rurales applied the "Ley Fuga" which meant the fugitive was "shot while trying to escape." Knowing all this, Doroteo mounted his horse and headed for the Sierra de la Silla. As a fugitive with a price on his head, he could not hide in the nearby villages where he would certainly be captured. Except for two or three attempts at making an honest living in the nearby towns, Doroteo spent most of the next 16 years, from age 16 to age 32, in the mountains of Chihuahua and Durango as a Robin Hood. Being a fugitive and always on the run, he rarely had an opportunity to visit his mother who lived in San Juan del Rio.

Within a few months of his escape from the hacienda, Doroteo was captured by three men who put him in jail in San Juan del Rio. The next morning Doroteo was told by his captors to

22

grind corn meal to make corn tortillas for breakfast. He saw this as an opportunity to make his escape. He took the metate stone (rock stone) for grinding corn and used it to kill one of the captors. He immediately started running on foot for the hills of Cerro Gordo and was able to complete his escape when he found a stray horse nearby. However, the stray horse soon tired and he had to continue on foot to the home of his cousin at Rio Grande, who provided him with a horse, saddle and some provisions. For the rest of the year, Doroteo stayed in the Sierra de la Silla and Sierra Gamon, an area where he was to find refuge while evading the Rurales, and years later hide many times while being pursued by General Pershing.

In October of 1895, Doroteo was almost captured when he was betrayed by a local villager named Pablo Martinez. He was asleep at the foot of Sierra de la Silla when he was awakened by seven men armed with rifles. Doroteo told the leader of the captors, Felix Sariana, that since there was no hurry, why not cook some ears of corn. Sariana agreed, but they had not noticed that Doroteo had his gun hidden under his pillow-blanket, and his horse and saddle were hidden nearby out of sight. While two men fetched corn ears and two others went for firewood, he pulled out his gun and starting shooting at the three remaining men, who immediately scattered for cover. By the time the seven captors regrouped, Doroteo was well on his way to his hideout.

Some three months later, he came close to being captured again by another posse. However, this time he could see the posse as they approached his hiding place. Since he knew the area quite well, he led the captors into an ambush. He took good aim and shot three men and some horses. When the pursuers scattered he made good his escape by a route that was only known to him. For the next five months, Doroteo spent his time in Sierra de Gamon where he slaughtered stolen cattle. He used the dry meat and skins to barter for coffee, beans, and other provisions with lumbermen who were cutting timber nearby.

It was at this point in his life that Doroteo decided to change his name to Pancho Villa. There are a number of legends as to why he adopted the name "Pancho Villa." One legend has it that the leader of the band he joined was known as "Pancho Villa." When the leader was mortally wounded and later died, the other members lamented the loss of their leader and wondered what was going to happen to them. At this precise moment, Doroteo stood up and shouted that Pancho Villa was not dead because, "I am Pancho Villa," and the group agreed to have him as their new leader. The legend sounds plausible, but there is no evidence to support that this claim is anywhere near the truth.

According to his memoirs, as dictated to Martin Guzman, the name Villa was adopted from his grandfather, whose name was Agustin Villa. Unfortunately, since there is no reliable historical account for the years he was a bandolero in the mountains, it is reasonable to rely on his memoirs regarding his early years because it resonates with a degree of truth.

Late in 1896, Villa returned to Sierra de la Silla to visit his friend, Jesus Alday, who lived at the Hacienda Santa Isabel de Berros. Alday informed Villa that he was a wanted man with a price on his head. Alday suggested that Villa join the bandit group of Ignacio Parra and Refugio Alvarado, who were more experienced, and perhaps, in this way, he could avoid being captured. When he met his new partners, they were not impressed since Villa was only a young man of perhaps 17 or 18 years of age. They asked him if he was sure that he wanted to join up because it would be a hard life as a bandit and he would have to obey their orders. Villa answered that he was already a wanted man so there was nothing to lose and he was prepared to do his part as a member of the group.

The next day on way to the small village of Tejame they ran into a herd of mules. Villa was told to remove the ringing bell from the lead mare and herd the mules to a holding area. From Tejame, it took them two or three days to reach the village of Ojito, where Parra and Alvarado had a connection with Don Ramon. There they rested for several days until the mules were sold. The stolen mules netted Villa 100 pesos, which was more money that he had ever seen before. With his share of the bounty he bought a new set of clothes. Before they left for their next adventure, they told Villa to get a good horse and saddle because, as a bandit, the saddle would be a good investment and his horse would be his best friend. Villa passed by a local saloon where he observed a fine horse and saddle. Without hesitation, he mounted the horse and took it to where they had previously hidden the herd of mules. The next day, when he rejoined the group they wanted to know how he had acquired such a fine horse. Villa said he got the horse from a drunk who had left the horse unattended at the saloon. Parra and Alvarado were impressed with this accomplishment and from then on his companions showed him more respect. Later in life Villa's inclination to commandeer beautiful horses would almost cost him his life.

When the group returned to his hometown of San Juan del Rio, Villa was able to visit and gave his Mother the few pesos he had left. She expressed deep concern because he had become a bandit and a fugitive. He answered that he really did not have a choice because he was a wanted man who was being persecuted by the Rurales who were controlled by the Hacendados (land barons). The following day, the group left for a ranch near Cantalan, where Parra had family. They were there only one day when a large posse of Rurales arrived in the morning to arrest Parra. As soon as the Rurales arrived, gunshots were exchanged and the group made their escape for Cerros de la Cocina. In the exchange of gunfire Alvarado's horse was shot from under him, but Villa returned and had Alvarado double mount with him. After their escape they stayed in the village of Pueblo Nuevo for three months, where Parra had a good friend who was a rich miner. When Parra learned that a cache of 150,000 pesos was on the way to the mine, they planned a highway holdup. After two days of waiting, they spotted the messenger with the 150,000 pesos. They jumped the money carrier, who was too frightened to reach for his gun. They found only 40,000 pesos in his jacket pocket and they left without harming the carrier.

As soon as they left, Villa told Parra that maybe the money was hidden somewhere in the saddle bags. Parra told Villa to return right away and there he found the remaining 110,000 pesos. They kept the carrier hostage for the night and the next day they divided the bounty and each one received 50,000 pesos.

With this good fortune, Villa returned to San Juan del Rio to visit his mother. He gave her 5,000 pesos and another 40,000 pesos was distributed among friends. He bought a tailor shop for his friend Antonio Retana and since Retana had very poor eyesight, he also hired a manager to run the tailor shop.

Early in 1898, Villa and the group decided to visit his mother at San Juan del Rio. The next day some 60 Rurales arrived to capture Villa. As soon as they saw the Rurales, they grabbed their rifles and exchanged gunfire. Felix Sariana, who had already captured Villa once before, was killed in the gunfire. Once again, they made their escape and headed for Sierra de Gamon. While asleep at the Sierra de Gamon, they were surprised by three deer hunters who were pointing rifles at them. The bandit group quickly drew their guns and shot the three pursuers. In the gunfire exchange, Alvarado was shot in the leg and Villa was grazed with a bullet to the chest. The group then moved to Sierra de la Silla for three months for Alvarado's leg to mend. Next, they moved near the village of Santiago Papasquiaro where they had some friends. Here they rustled some 300 head of cattle to be slaughtered and sold in Tejame by their good friend, Don Julio. Parra told Villa and Alvarado to deliver the pack of mules loaded with dried meat to Don Julio. On the way down the mountain road Villa lost one of the mules and for this Alvarado vociferously cursed Villa and his family. Villa became incensed and pulled his rifle and in the exchange of gunfire he shot Alvarado's horse in the forehead. Alvarado and the horse went tumbling down the mountain slope. When Alvarado hit bottom, he had lost his rifle and begged Villa not to shoot him. Villa returned to their hideout and informed Parra of the trouble with Alvarado.

Parra left to find Alvarado and when he returned he told Villa that Alvarado was no longer a member of the group, meaning Parra got rid of Alvarado. Next they went to Durango to visit a lady friend of Parra's. While there they quickly realized they had been betrayed by a local villager when Jesus Flores and another man arrived wanting to know the identity of Parra and Villa. Again, there was an exchange of gunfire, Jesus Flores fell dead, and they made their escape to Sierra de la Silla.

Sometime later, José Solis, a friend of Parra, joined up with the group. On the way to Cantalan, they came upon an old man with a mule and two boxes with bread. Solis asked the old man to sell him some bread, but the old man refused, saying the bread was for the owner of the hacienda. Solis told the old man that if he did not sell the bread he would take it from him. The old man said, "In my affairs, only I command" Solis killed him by shooting him twice. Villa protested to Parra that it wasn't necessary to kill the old man. Parra retorted that the old man didn't have to die if only he had given up the bread. Villa told Parra that if things were not going to change, he would leave the group. Parra told him, leave if you like, but you won't survive without me. Villa left and returned to San Juan del Rio, where he stayed hidden for two months at the home of Antonio Retana, the tailor whom he set up in business.

Villa left to visit family at the Hacienda de Menores. On the way he took a path that cut across the Hacienda owned by Don Eulogio Veloz. There he was stopped by a horseman who accused him of trespassing and said he would take him to the owner. As the horseman approached, he struck Villa with a horse whip, whence Villa became angry, pulled his gun, and killed the horseman. Villa lamented the fact that if the man had not struck him and accused him of trespassing, he would still be alive. At the Hacienda de Menores he became acquainted with Manuel Torres, where they learned that a certain Catarino Saldana would be transporting 1,000 pesos. Villa and Torres laid in wait, robbed Saldana, and divided the 1,000 pesos. Villa left his share in trust with family members. Torres later returned to the home of the family with a fraudulent note saying that they should give Villa's money and his two horses to Torres. Villa pursued Torres until he found him at the Hacienda los Menores. He was about to kill him but he changed his mind when Torres begged for his life. While at the village of Tejame near the Hacienda Los Menores, Villa was paid a visit by two Rurales who came to arrest him. Villa shot the two Rurales and headed for the mountains of Durango.

When Villa took to the mountains, all the injustices and inequities of the campesinos that he experienced as a teenager now became a reality. He would no longer have the opportunity to grow into a peaceful adulthood and perhaps to leave the Hacienda to find a wife, a job, and a better life. The doors for all his dreams and aspirations were now closed forever. At age sixteen he became a fugitive with a price on his head and once he left the San Juan del Rio, there was no turning back. Villa lived during a period when the wealthy gained more wealth and the poor stayed poor. In the wilderness of the mountains he could recount the conquest of the Spaniards who for three hundred years plundered the land for gold and silver to be sent to Mother Spain; the near slavery and exploitation of Indian Civilizations; and the introduction of Catholicism as the omnipotent religion whose destiny was to replace the ancient rituals of the indigenous people of the land before Cortes. He became of age during the dynasty of Porfirio Diaz, who was imbued with a European mentality favoring foreigners and French customs and architecture.

By the time Villa joined the Revolution in 1910 he had become a hardened human being who had no respect for the law, if the law served to punish the disenfranchised. When he was recruited, the Revolutionary leaders knew of his exploits as a renegade bandit and yet they offered him the rank of Captain. This then was Pancho Villa, the uneducated and illiterate guerilla warrior who had no training in military affairs. He was a born leader who once he joined the Revolution, was brutal, ruthless, unforgiving, and vindictive against those who would betray him.

Some areas where Doroteo Arango went into hiding before he became Pancho Villa.

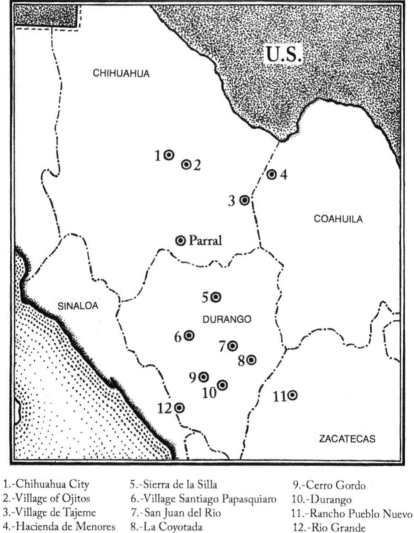

1.-Chihuahua City	5.-Sierra de la Silla	9.-Cerro Gordo
2.-Village of Ojitos	6.-Village Santiago Papasquiaro	10.-Durango
3.-Village de Tajeme	7.-San Juan del Rio	11.-Rancho Pueblo Nuevo
4.-Hacienda de Menores	8.-La Coyotada	12.-Rio Grande

Chapter II.   Five Revolutions for the Price of One

Mexican historians have established November 20, 1910, as the starting date of the Mexican Revolution. On that day, while in exile in San Antonio, Texas, Francisco Madero proclaimed he was the rightful heir to the Presidency and issued a call to his compatriots to revolt against the regime of President Porfirio Diaz. The Revolution devastated the nation, claimed over one million lives, and involved high level treason, a number of plots and subplots by the Revolutionaries to assume the leadership of the nation, and preemptive military intervention by the United States.

When Madero called for a Revolution, never in his wildest dreams could he have imagined he had unleashed a chain of events that would keep the nation in turmoil for ten years. He could not have foreseen, nor could the world have foreseen, the emergence of tyrants ambitious for power as well as American diplomatic intervention, invasion, and military occupation. Before it was over, the nation was consumed by five separate and distinct Revolutions: the removal of President Porfirio Diaz from the Presidency; the Revolt by General Emiliano Zapata; the Revolt by General Pascual Orozco against the Presidency of Madero; the wrongful assumption of the Presidency by General Victoriano Huerta; and the bitter conflict between General Francisco "Pancho" Villa and Primer Jefe Venustiano Carranza to assume leadership of the nation.

The First Conflict – Removal of President Diaz

By the time of the 1910 elections, Porfirio Diaz, who was eighty years old, had been President of Mexico for over thirty years. In 1908, in a newspaper interview with an American journalist of *Pearson's Magazine*, President Diaz stated that he would not run for another term of office. The country at last believed the Dictatorship of Diaz would come to an end, but later Diaz changed his mind about the presidency when he announced that Ramon Corral was his choice for Vice President. The reversal on the part of Diaz incensed the leaders of the nation who wanted the Diaz Dictatorship to come to an end. Enter Francisco Madero, a wealthy landowner from the State of Coahuila who would campaign against the reelection of Diaz. In 1910, Madero wrote a book, *Presidential Succession*, to oppose the national malaise of having a President serve unending consecutive terms. Madero also embarked on a political campaign of "Elected Suffrage and No Reelection" to gain support for his Presidential candidacy. When it appeared that Madero would win the election, Diaz had him arrested and sent to prison.

When the elections were over, as predictable, Diaz was again re-elected President. Madero escaped from jail and took refuge in San Antonio, Texas, where he wrote the Plan de San Luis Potosi. Madero claimed he had legitimately won the Presidency and that President Diaz had to be removed. Madero called for the nation to start the Revolution on November 20, 1910. In the ensuing months, Pancho Villa, Pascual Orozco, and Emiliano Zapata won a number of important battles for Madero, the most important being the battle for Ciudad Juarez on May 27, 1911. The defeat of the Federal Army at Ciudad Juarez brought about the Treaty of Juarez, whereby President Diaz agreed to resign the Presidency and leave Mexico to live in Paris, France. With the departure of Diaz, the Revolution had achieved its main purpose, the removal of Diaz from the Presidency. After thirty years of dictatorship it appeared the nation could now move forward with the social and land reforms that Villa and Zapata had fought for. But this was not to be, for no one had anticipated the revolt by Emiliano Zapata and Pascual Orozco, and the betrayal of General Victoriano Huerta against President Madero.

The Second Conflict – Revolt by General Emiliano Zapata

Soon after Madero assumed the Presidency, Zapata called for a meeting with him to discuss agrarian land reform in the State of Morelos. Zapata informed Madero that his people joined the Revolution because they expected Madero would take action for the return of their ancestral lands that had been wrongfully confiscated. Zapata had been fighting since 1908 for the return of the land that had been confiscated by the large sugar cane land barons. For years, the Hacendados had been encroaching on lands owned by the villagers by cutting off irrigation water and filing questionable lawsuits. Eventually, the villagers lost so much land, that they had to go to work for the Hacendados as peonage workers.

Now that the Revolution was over, they wanted action and not political promises. Unfortunately, Madero informed Zapata that land reform would take time because new legislation had to be introduced and approved by the Mexican Congress. Zapata was upset by Madero's lack of response. Instead of being responsive, Madero informed Zapata he should lay down his arms and deactivate his army. Zapata considered Madero's request an insult to the aims of the Revolution. Madero failed to understand that Zapata had been fighting for land reform for years, even before he agreed to join the Revolution against Diaz.

Zapata became disillusioned and declared he was now in open rebellion against the Madero Presidency. Matters became more complicated when Provisional President de la Barra, with the concurrence of Madero, initiated an ill-advised military campaign to pacify Zapata, a campaign that was entrusted to General Victoriano Huerta, an old crusty general under the Diaz regime. While Madero continued to pursue reconciliation with Zapata, Huerta was leading a determined military campaign throughout the states of Morelos and Puebla to capture and imprison Zapata.

The Third Conflict – Revolt by General Pascual Orozco

After Madero was installed as the President of Mexico, Villa retired to private life in the State of Chihuahua with the rank of Colonel, and Orozco was given command of the Rurales in Chihuahua. Orozco was not satisfied with his new assignment because what he really coveted was the position of Secretary of War, a position that was given to Venustiano Carranza.

Under the Diaz Administration large landowners were not required to pay taxes. Madero correctly ordered that henceforth the Hacendados were to pay their share of taxes, as well as back taxes. The Hacendados were naturally opposed to Madero's mandate on taxes because they wanted to return to the good old days when they received preferential treatment under the Diaz regime. Knowing Orozco's discontent, the wealthy Hacendados and newspaper giant William Randolph Hearst sought him out to revolt against the Madero Presidency.

On March 1, 1912, once Orozco knew he had the financial support of the Hacendados, he openly declared against the Madero Presidency in the State of Chihuahua. To gain support for his revolt, Orozco adopted the catchy phrase of "Tierra y Justicia"

(Land and Justice). His troops used red flags and called themselves "Los Colorados." To defeat the Colorados, Madero designated General Victoriano Huerta as the Commander of all military forces in Chihuahua. Huerta in turn requested that President Madero recall Villa with the rank of Brigadier General. Since Orozco did not want Villa to fight on the side of Madero, he offered Villa 300,000 pesos to leave for the U.S. Villa answered that he would not accept any amount of money because he was not a traitor. On another occasion, Orozco sent an emissary to Villa's wife Luz Corral to offer him amnesty if he would give up his fight against Orozco. Luz Corral answered that she would rather live in poverty than live with a turncoat.

In the first few weeks of the revolt, with the support of the Hacendados and the well-to-do, it appeared Orozco was going to achieve victory. The Orozco rebellion ran out of steam when the U.S. Senate and House of Representatives convinced President William Howard Taft to institute an embargo of weapons to all revolutionary forces in Mexico. The embargo was easily circumvented by Madero by buying armaments from Europe that could be delivered at the Port of Veracruz. Orozco, on the other hand, could not overcome the American arms blockade because his military operations were confined to the State of Chihuahua, a land locked area that did not have access to a seaport for importing munitions from Europe.

The Orozco revolt came to an end on May 22, 1912, when Huerta and Villa decisively defeated Orozco's Colorados in the battle for Rellano, in the vicinity of Jimenez. After his defeat, Orozco escaped to live in the U.S. But this was not the end of Orozco. A few months later Orozco would reunite with Huerta, after Huerta had wrongfully assumed the Presidency. Orozco became a General under Huerta and would go on to command his former brigade – Los Colorados.

The Fourth Conflict – Assassination of Madero

Although Francisco Madero conducted a brilliant military campaign to remove President Diaz, his own Presidency lasted only fifteen months. Once Madero had achieved victory, he made a number of critical mistakes that led to his downfall: he failed to assume the Presidency as soon as Diaz was removed; he retained many Diaz cronies in office; he permitted many of his adversaries to plot against his Presidency; he failed to reach an accord with Emiliano Zapata, and he vested excessive military power in General Victoriano Huerta. Most importantly he failed to adequately assess the complicity between General Huerta and U.S. Ambassador Henry Lane Wilson to destroy his Presidency.

According to the Plan de San Luis Potosi (Madero's plan to start the Revolution), Madero was to become the Provisional President as soon as Diaz was defeated (May 27, 1911). However, instead of immediately assuming the Presidency, Madero agreed to have Francisco Leon de la Barra, a Diplomat under the Diaz regime, to serve as the Interim President from June to November 1911, a period of five months. By not taking firm control of the nation's political affairs during these crucial months, Madero provided his adversaries with a five month window of opportunity to plot against his administration. From a political perspective, his biggest mistake was his inability to reach an accord with the demands by Zapata for the immediate return of ancestral lands to the campesinos in the State of Morelos. Instead of being responsive, Madero informed Zapata that it would take time to implement land reform; in the meantime, he should lay down his arms and deactivate his army. Having been rebuked by Madero, Zapata declared he was now in open rebellion against the Madero Presidency. Matters became more complicated when Provisional President de la Barra, with the concurrence of Madero,

36

initiated a military campaign against Zapata, a campaign that was assigned to General Victoriano Huerta, an alcoholic general under the Diaz regime.

The final blow for Madero was his failure to counteract the overt actions of U.S. Ambassador Henry Lane Wilson, an outspoken critic of Madero, and the plotting of Generals Victoriano Huerta, Bernardo Reyes, and Felix Diaz, nephew of Porfirio Diaz. Ambassador Wilson, a holdover from the Taft Presidency, was not a friend of Madero. Ambassador Wilson openly aided the conspiracy being orchestrated by Huerta, Felix Diaz, and Bernardo Reyes to remove Madero from office. He sent untruthful communiques to the State Department stating that Madero was incompetent, that he was disliked by foreign representatives, and that he did not have the support from the nation's constituency. On February 18, 1913, Huerta ordered the arrest of Madero and Vice President Pino Suarez. They were first imprisoned in Mexico City and later told they were being transferred to another location for their safety. When the time came to be transferred, they were placed in an automobile, and as they left the prison grounds they were assassinated by claiming La Ley Fuga, or shot while attempting to escape. As soon as Madero and Suarez were assassinated, Huerta immediately claimed the Presidency by coercing the Mexican Congress to declare him as the President of Mexico.

Huerta's Presidency only lasted seventeen months. By July 1914, he was defeated by the forces of Venustiano Carranza, Pablo Gonzalez, Alvaro Obregon, and Pancho Villa operating in the Northern States of Mexico, and Zapata who operated in the South in the State of Morelos, only sixty miles from Mexico City. Final defeat came to General Huerta's Federal army when he lost the battles for the cities of Ciudad Juarez, Chihuahua City, Saltillo,

Torreon, and finally the battle for Zacatecas, the railroad gateway to Mexico City. After Huerta resigned the Presidency on July 8, 1914, he was taken to the Port of Veracruz to leave immediately for Spain on the German ship *Ypiranga*.

The Fifth Conflict – Conflict between Villa and Carranza

On the surface, during the campaign to remove Huerta, Generals Villa, Zapata, Carranza, and Obregón appeared to be united. In the north, Villa was wining great battles in the states of Chihuahua and Durango; Carranza and Obregón were wining battles in the states of Jalisco and Sonora. In the south, Zapata was victorious in his home state of Morelos. Although the Generals of the Revolution appeared to be unified, there developed a chasm between the forces of Villa and Carranza because Carranza wanted total control over Villa's army of the north. On the other hand, Villa did not trust Carranza and did not agree with his mandate for total subjugation of his army, "La Gran Division del Norte" because Villa maintained that his army was an independent army, supplied and paid for by Villa.

Carranza failed to recognize that when he unilaterally assumed the leadership of the nation as Primer Jefe, it was a temporary measure until formal elections could be conducted, nor was he explicit that he would have total control over all military operations. Despite the fact that Carranza was operating on a narrow mandate, he nonetheless, insisted that Villa become totally subordinate to his authority. The conflict between the two generals became magnified when plans were being made to take the City of Zacatecas, the last stronghold of the Huerta regime.

With some 20,000 troops Villa planned to take Zacatecas and immediately move on to Mexico City. Carranza was well aware that if Villa arrived in Mexico City first, his standing as the Primer

Jefe, and leader of Mexico, would be severely weakened. To prevent Villa from moving on Mexico City, Carranza ordered Villa to attack the City of Saltillo. To attack Saltillo, Villa would have to move 150 miles to the east, when in fact he was moving in a southerly direction. Villa refused the order because Saltillo was in the sector assigned to General Pablo Gonzalez.

After Villa refused, Carranza ordered Villa to loan General Panfilo Natera 5,000 soldiers. Again, Villa refused because he did not believe that General Natera had the ability to secure a victory at Saltillo. Eventually, in an effort to reconcile with Carranza, Villa successfully attacked Saltillo and made plans to attack the fortified City of Zacatecas. This time Carranza denied Villa the coal supplies that he had promised to provide and that Villa needed to move his troop trains against Zacatecas. Due to the delay by Villa in taking Zacatecas, Alvaro Obregon, Carranza's favorite general, was able to march triumphantly into Mexico City first.

After the defeat of Huerta, the Revolutionaries called for the Convention of Aguascalientes in the State of Aguascalientes. After several days of bickering, the Revolutionary leaders voted to remove Carranza as Primer Jefe, and selected Eulalio Gutierrez as Provisional President until formal elections for President could be held. Carranza did not agree with the outcome and rejected the decision of the Convention. Since the leadership question was not resolved, the convention ended in two divided camps; the Constitutionalists for Carranza and Obregón, who believed they were acting according the Constitution of Mexico, and the Conventionists for Villa and Zapata, who believed they were upholding the outcome of the Aguascalientes Convention, and thus the aims of the Revolution. After the Aguascalientes Convention, Villa and Carranza engaged in life and death battles for the leadership of the nation where no quarter was given and few prisoners were taken.

Since the start of the Revolution, Villa's military tactics of an all-out frontal attack brought him many victories (to start a major attack, Villa would always implore his soldiers to deliver "Un Golpe Terrifico"). On the other hand, General Obregón had studied the tactics of warfare taking place in Europe, and he had on his staff a number of German officers with experience fighting in the trenches of World War I. General Obregón learned how to defend against cavalry charges by employing trenches, barbed wire, and registering interdicting machine gun fire at the point of the assault. These improvements in warfare proved fatal for Villa in the battle for the City of Celaya, in the State of Guanajuato.

On April 6, 1915, Villa ordered a frontal attack on the City of Celaya, where he lost 5,000 Villistas. He attacked Celaya again on April 13, and lost another 3,000 Villistas.

Although Villa lost the battle of Celaya in April, and later at Agua Prieta, in the State of Sonora, in the following year he mounted several successful campaigns in the State of Chihuahua where he continued to keep Carranza on the defensive.

The conflict between Villa and Carranza prolonged the Revolution for another five years, until 1920. Villa was given amnesty, and he retired to his ranch, El Canutillo, in the State of Durango, near the City of Parral.

Turning Points of the Revolution

1910

- When President Diaz recognizes he will be defeated for the Presidency, he orders the arrest of Francisco Madero.

- On November 20, 1910 Francisco Madero declares a Revolution against President Diaz.

1911

- Madero becomes first democratically elected President of Mexico in thirty years.

- Emiliano Zapata revolts against Madero over the return of ancestral lands.

- Pascual Orozco revolts against Madero over patronage.

1913

- U.S. Ambassador Henry Lane Wilson conspires with General Huerta to remove President Madero

- In February, General Huerta orchestrates the assassination of President Madero for the purpose of assuming the Presidency of Mexico.

- In February, General Huerta wrongfully assumes the Presidency.

- Carranza declares himself Primer Jefe of Mexico for the purpose of removing General Huerta from the Presidency.

1914

- In April, the U.S. Atlantic Fleet conducts a naval blockade of the Port of Tampico

- On Aril 21, the U.S. Atlantic Fleet delivers 3,500 troops to occupy the Port of Veracruz

- General Huerta is defeated by the combined military forces of Villa, Zapata, Carranza, Obregón, and Gonzalez.

- In October, the Aguascalientes Convention is convened to decide the leadership of Mexico and elect a Provisional President.

- Eulalio Gutierrez is elected Provisional President of Mexico, but Carranza refuses to resign as Primer Jefe.

- Revolutionaries become divided into two factions, Villa and Zapata as the Conventionists against Carranza and Obregón as the Constitutionalists.

1915

- In April, Villa is decisively defeated in the battle for the City of Celaya.

- In October 19, President Wilson recognizes Carranza as de facto leader of Mexico, at the expense of Pancho Villa.

- In October, President Wilson authorizes the U.S. Army to use military trains to transport 5,000 Carranza troops on U.S. railways, from Eagles Pass, Texas to Douglas, Arizona, across the border from Agua Prieta. The Carranza troops arrive in time to defeat Villa in the battle for Agua Prieta.

1916

- Villa attacks Columbus, New Mexico in retaliation against President Wilson for providing direct military assistance to Carranza.

- President Wilson authorizes General Pershing to enter Mexico with over 10,000 U.S. Cavalry to capture Villa (The Punitive Expedition).

- The U.S. Army engages the Mexican Army in firefights in the towns of Parral and Chamizal, Chihuahua. This military action is contrary to the orders issued to General Pershing. General Pershing's orders are to capture Pancho Villa, not engage Carranza troops.

- To resolve the occupation of Mexico, President Wilson agrees to establish the "High Commission" to decide how the U.S. will depart from Mexico.

1917

- After one year in Mexico, General Pershing is unable to capture Pancho Villa and departs Mexico empty handed.

1918

- Pancho Villa's fortunes of war are revived and he continues fighting Carranza by capturing Torreon, Coahuila, and Chihuahua City.

1919

- Zapata is assassinated by order of Carranza in an ambush at the Hacienda Chinemeca in the State of Morelos.

- Felipe Ángeles is court martialed and executed by order of Carranza in the State of Chihuahua.

1920

- Carranza is forced to vacate the Presidency and is assassinated in Veracruz as he tries to leave Mexico.

- Villa receives amnesty from the government and retires from the Revolution at the Hacienda El Canutillo, a 25,000 acre ranch near Parral, Chihuahua.

1923

- Villa is assassinated while on a business trip at Parral, Chihuahua. He dies instantly when he is ambushed by eight assailants.

Chapter III. Death and Assassination of the Leaders of the Revolution

After the assassination of President Madero, and for the next seven years of the Revolution, several of the leading personalities changed sides or allegiance. The Revolution exacted a high price on the leadership of the Revolution. All the leading revolutionaries died tragically by assassination or died soon after the Revolution ended in 1920. These changes in leadership may cause the reader some confusion because at one moment they would be united, and the next, they were fighting against each other.

A brief description of the leading personalities is presented to clarify their role during the Revolution.

The Key Characters of the Revolution

(listed in alphabetical order)

General Felipe Ángeles

Felipe Ángeles was the right-hand man for Villa on military organizational matters and an expert on the use of artillery. Ángeles was born on June 13, 1868, in the State of Hidalgo, and attended the Military Academy at Chapultepec, in Mexico City. Throughout the Revolution, Ángeles gained a reputation as an honorable person with an astute military mind.

When the revolution broke out in 1910 against President Porfirio Diaz, Ángeles was still in France on a military assignment, and was unable to return to Mexico until 1912. When he returned to Mexico, he was appointed by President Madero as

Superintendent of the Military Academy at Chapultepec Castle. Under Madero, Ángeles was regarded as a dignified officer and a person of honor, and in June 1912 he was promoted to Brigadier General.

In 1913, when President Madero was removed from office and assassinated by General Huerta, Ángeles was arrested along with President Madero and Vice President Pino Suárez. However, Ángeles' life was spared because of his outstanding work in training the cadets of the Military Academy. That same year, when Carranza assumed leadership of Mexico, Ángeles was appointed as Secretary of War. Later he was relegated to Assistant Secretary of War because he did not have the support of the Carranza generals, who claimed that he had not fought in the Revolution to remove President Porfirio Diaz.

Since Ángeles was unhappy with his situation in Mexico City, in 1914 he was able to convince Carranza to transfer him to serve under Villa as an expert on artillery operations.

Ángeles was the architect of the greatest battles won by Villa in Chihuahua, Torreon, and Zacatecas, by using superior military tactics and superior artillery. By 1915, he was frustrated by his inability to influence Villa, as well as the destruction and carnage being caused by the Revolution, particularly after the Battle for Celaya, and in 1915 decided to immigrate to the United States. He returned to Chihuahua in 1918 to try to convince Villa to end the Revolution. Because he was not able to convince Villa, he decided to return to the United States. He was captured in the State of Chihuahua and sent to prison in Ciudad Juarez, where Carranza ordered that Ángeles be court martialed for being anti-government. He was tried by a military tribunal, even though he was in civilian clothing when captured and had been out of the Revolution for three years, living in the United States.

Ángeles was executed before a firing squad on November 29, 1919. On the day of his execution, Ángeles made an impassioned speech on the aims of the Revolution and how the day would come when Mexico would be rid of dictators and tyrants.

President Venustiano Carranza

In 1913, following the assassination of President Madero, Venustiano Carranza joined with Generals Villa, Zapata, Obregón, and González to remove General Victoriano Huerta, who had gained the Presidency by betrayal. During the first part of his presidency, Carranza made many constructive changes to improve the education system and bring about land reform. However, towards the end of his presidency he was more concerned with accumulating wealth.

For the 1920 election, by constitutional law, Carranza could not be reelected. He nonetheless wanted to retain power and decided to support Ignacio Bonillas, an unknown candidate. Most observers believed that he would support General Alvaro Obregon, who had declared his candidacy for the Presidency, and who had been his loyal general throughout the Revolution. When Carranza learned that his efforts to install Bonillas would fail, he tried to have Obregon arrested, but Obregon escaped to the State of Guerrero. When Carranza realized that the supporters of Obregon had turned against him, he decided to leave Mexico. His plan was to leave from the Port of Veracruz. When he arrived at the small village of Tlaxcalantongo, Puebla, he was betrayed by Colonel Rodolfo Herrero, who had him assassinated on May 21, 1920.

President Porfirio Diaz

Porfirio Diaz was President of Mexico for over thirty years, from 1876 to 1910. He ruled the country as a dictator, had a

European mentality, and looked down on his own people. In 1910, he was challenged by Francisco Madero for the Presidency. When it was clear that Madero would win the election, Diaz had him sent to prison. Madero escaped to San Antonio, Texas, and from there he called for a revolt against Diaz. The armies of Madero defeated Diaz in May 1911, in Ciudad Juarez.

President Diaz was escorted to Veracruz by General Huerta, and he left Mexico for France aboard the German ship *Ypiranga*. Four years later, Diaz died in Paris, France, on July 3, 1915.

General Rodolfo Fierro

Rodolfo Fierro was a former railroad worker in the State of Sonora. When he joined the Revolution, Fierro provided Villa with two essential assets: his expertise on the use of railroads for military operations and his role in serving as Villa's right hand man enforcing discipline and executing prisoners.

Fierro met his death on October 14, 1915, in the State of Chihuahua. Fierro was on a mission for Villa near Casas Grandes when he ran into some muddy water which turned out to be quicksand at the Casas Grandes Lagoon.

General Victoriano Huerta

Victoriano Huerta became a military general in the Federal Army under the Diaz regime. He was a competent but ruthless general who employed severe military tactics against the Indians of Yucatan. In February 1913, General Huerta assumed the Presidency after he ordered the assassinations of President Madero and Vice President Pino Suárez. As soon as General Huerta assumed the Presidency, he was opposed by Carranza, Villa, Zapata, and Obregón. General Huerta lost successive battles in the cities of Saltillo, Torreon, and Zacatecas. With the loss of

Zacatecas, General Huerta knew he was defeated and left Mexico to live in Spain. He returned in 1915 to restart the Revolution, but he was captured in the State of New Mexico by the U.S. Government. He was sent to prison at El Paso, Texas, where he suffered from the effects of alcoholism. He was allowed to live in Texas with his family, where he died in July 1915.

President Francisco Madero

In November 1911, Madero became the President of Mexico, but his Presidency lasted only fifteen months because he was not politically astute. He allowed members of the Diaz regime to plot against him and he did not adequately respond to Emiliano Zapata's request for land reform. On February 18, 1913, Madero was sent to prison by generals loyal to former President Diaz. The conspirators were led by Generals Victoriano Huerta, Felix Diaz (nephew of Porfirio Diaz), and Bernardo Reyes. They were also assisted by the covert intervention of U.S. Ambassador Henry Lane Wilson.

President Madero and Vice President Pino Suárez resigned when they were led to believe by the conspirators that their lives, as well as the lives of their families, would be spared. Madero and Suarez were assassinated on February 22, 1912. They were told they were being removed from prison for their own safety, but this was a ruse to assassinate them as soon as they left the prison grounds.

President Alvaro Obregón.

Alvaro Obregón was born on February 19, 1880, in Navajoa, Sonora. In 1910, during the first part of the Revolution, Obregón was not active in Madero's effort to remove Porfirio Diaz. He became active after Madero was assassinated when Obregón joined forces with Pancho Villa, Emiliano Zapata, and Venustiano Carranza to remove General Huerta.

From a military point of view, Obregón was perhaps the most competent general of the Revolution. He consistently won military battles, successfully employed the Yaqui Indians from his state of Sonora to fight as brave warriors, and employed superior military tactics. His most outstanding victory was against Pancho Villa in the battle for the City of Celaya, in the State of Guanajuato.

Obregón was elected President in 1920, and his administration was considered progressive. However, he made many enemies when he took drastic measures against the Catholic Church. After his first Presidency, Obregón wanted to be elected President again, but according to the Constitution of Mexico, he could not run for a second consecutive term. He waited until 1928, to campaign for the Presidency. Despite Catholic opposition, Obregón won the election, but before he could take office, he was assassinated on July 17, 1928, by José de Leon Toral, a devout Roman Catholic.

General Pancho Villa

Pancho Villa, the son of sharecroppers, became the head of the family at age 15 when his father died. At age 16 he shot the son of the owner of the Hacienda for having molested his sister, Martinita. He was forced to flee into the mountains of the State of Chihuahua to avoid incarceration. For 16 years he lived as a fugitive, until the start of the Revolution. In 1910, at the age of 32 he was recruited to serve as a military leader. He formed his own army, La Gran Division del Norte, and commanded as many as 50,000 soldiers.

Villa fought in the Revolution for ten years. In 1920, Villa was given amnesty by the Mexican Government. He was awarded the

Hacienda El Canutillo; a 25,000 acre ranch located 45 miles from Parral, and was authorized 50 of his beloved Dorados de Villa as his personal escort at government expense.

On July 19, 1923, Villa was in Parral, Chihuahua to attend to business matters. He left Parral on the morning of July 20, by automobile. When his automobile slowed to make a turn at Gabino Barrera Street, he was ambushed by eight of his enemies. Villa and four of his escorts were killed instantly.

General Emiliano Zapata

After 1914, Carranza troops made many attempts to capture the elusive Zapata in his home state of Morelos. Five years later, in 1919, Carranza ordered General Pablo Gonzalez to invade Morelos to make a determined effort to destroy the army of Zapata. Although General Gonzalez had a superior military force, he was unable to capture the wily guerilla warrior. In April 1919, General Gonzalez received information that one of his subordinates, Colonel Jesus Guajardo, had disobeyed orders when it was reported he was in a cantina instead of chasing Zapata. General Gonzalez did not punish Colonel Guajardo but did place him under close scrutiny by his commander. When Zapata learned that Guajardo was in trouble with his commanders he sent him a secret message asking him to switch sides and join his army.

The secret message was intercepted by General Gonzalez, who set up a plan to assassinate Zapata. The plan was for Colonel Guajardo to relay to Zapata that he would take his army unit with him and join Zapata's army. Colonel Guajardo and Zapata agreed to meet at the Hacienda Chinemeca.

When Zapata arrived at Hacienda Chinemeca, he was met by an Honor Guard, but this was a ruse. As soon as Zapata arrived, the Honor Guard turned their rifles on Zapata and killed him instantly. For his deceptive and devious action, Colonel Guajardo was promoted to General and the 50,000 pesos reward he received was distributed among the "Honor Guard" that assassinated Zapata.

Emiliano Zapata was 39 years old when he was assassinated.

Chapter IV. Pictorial Review of the Revolutionary Leaders

President Porfirio Diaz

Dictator of Mexico for over thirty years who ruled the nation with an iron fist. Provided preferential treatment for U.S. and European investors in land ownership, processing natural resources, and oil exploration. Deposed in 1911 by Francisco Madero. Died in Paris, France in 1915, at age 85.

Los Cientificos

President Diaz's cabinet members. Along with President Diaz, all became wealthy by allowing United States and European investors to make lucrative investments in Mexico. Failed to develop a Mexican middle class to govern the country.

President Francisco Madero

President of Mexico from 1911 to 1913. His Presidency lasted only fifteen months. He was not strong enough to neutralize his adversaries and the army generals who had served under the Diaz Dictatorship. President Madero and Vice President Pino Suarez were assassinated on February 22, 1913, by a group of Mexican Army Generals under the guidance of General Victoriano Huerta.

55

Henry Lane Wilson

U.S. Ambassador to Mexico under the President Taft Administration. He was opposed to the Presidency of Francisco Madero. Ambassador Wilson conspired with Mexican Army Generals to have President Madero arrested and eventually assassinated. Ambassador Wilson urged President Woodrow Wilson to recognize Huerta as the President of Mexico.

Woodrow Wilson

President of the U.S. during most of the period of the Mexican Revolution of 1910. He ordered the invasion of the Port of Tampico, the occupation of the Port of Veracruz, provided military aid to transport the Mexican Army of Carranza, and ordered Gen. Pershing to capture Pancho Villa.

General Victoriano Huerta

Was the leader of the Mexican Army Generals that conspired to remove and assassinate President Madero. His Presidency lasted only sixteen months. Pancho Villa, Emiliano Zapata, Pablo Gonzalez, Alvaro Obregon, and Venustiano Carranza joined forces to remove Huerta from the Presidency.

General Francisco "Pancho" Villa

General Villa was the leader of the Gran Division del Norte, the most powerful army of the Mexican Revolution. Born in rural Mexico to sharecropper parents. Became a fugitive, at age sixteen when he shot the landlord for molesting his fourteen year old sister. Avoided capture by Gen. Pershing of the U.S. Army. Retired from the Revolution in 1920, when he was granted amnesty. Was assassinated in Parral, Chihuahua in 1923. He died at age forty-five.

General Felipe Angeles

An articulate and intelligent military officer trained at the Chapultepec Military Academy. Planned the greatest battles won by the Army of Pancho Villa. In 1916, he went to live in the United States. When he returned to Chihuahua in 1918 to convince Pancho Villa to bring the Revolution to an end, he was captured by Carranza troops. He was court martialed and executed by firing squad in 1919.

Venustiano Carranza

Served as a Senator during the Diaz Presidency. Elected as Governor of the State of Coahuila. After President Madero was assassinated, he installed himself as the Primer Jefe of Mexico. Engaged in a protracted dispute with Pancho Villa for the leadership of Mexico. The nation turned against him when he tried to control the 1920 Presidential Election. He was assassinated in 1920.

General Pascual Orozco

One of the leading generals under Madero to remove President Diaz. He revolted against President Diaz when he was not appointed as Minister of War. He was defeated in 1912 in the State of Chihuahua by Pancho Villa and Victoriano Huerta.

Rodolfo Fierro

Right hand man for Pancho Villa regarding execution of prisoners. A daring leader of the Dorados de la Division del Norte, an expert on railroads and the use of explosives

Obregon, Villa, and Pershing

At one time, they were the three amigos. They met at El Paso, Texas when the Revolution was at a high pitch to remove General Huerta. Years later, Obregon and Villa would be bitter enemies, and Gen. Pershing was ordered to capture Villa in 1916.

Chapter V.   Villa Joins the Revolution

By 1910, President Porfirio Diaz had ruled Mexico for over thirty years. He had been elected to office seven times, and under his regime no one could be elected as a governor of a state or elected to the Mexican Congress without his approval. A year earlier, in 1909, President Diaz in an interview with the American newspaperman James Creelman stated he would not seek reelection for the 1910 presidency, but the next year, at age 80, he changed his mind and declared that he would seek another term. Some people believed the announcement by Diaz was a ploy to discourage any opposition. Diaz failed to realize that many leaders in Mexico were tired of his dictatorship and were prepared to challenge him for the Presidency.

Bernardo Reyes, Governor of the State of Tamaulipas and a crony of Diaz, wanted to become President because he believed that Diaz would die in office. Francisco Madero, a wealthy landowner from the State of Coahuila, firmly believed the nation was entitled to open democratic elections to end the Diaz dictatorship. Reyes was eliminated as a candidate when he was sent by Diaz as a special envoy to France. Madero gained national support for his candidacy when he wrote *"Presidential Succession,"* a book calling for free elections and open government. Madero also established several "Non reelection" political committees that attracted many followers throughout the country. By 1910, Madero had raised the level of awareness for the nation to vote against the reelection of Diaz. As Madero gained momentum and when it became clear that he would win the presidency, Diaz had him arrested and imprisoned in the federal prison in San Luis

Potosi in the State of San Luis Potosi. While in prison, Madero wrote the Plan of San Luis Potosi, calling for an end to continuous re-elections by the party in power. Madero escaped from prison to live in San Antonio, Texas, and from there he called for a Revolution to start against Diaz on November 20, 1910 (the official date of the start of the Mexican Revolution).

Loyalty to Francisco Madero

Madero planned to start the Revolution by entering the State of Chihuahua, and once in Chihuahua, he hoped to gain momentum and gather recruits as he travelled south towards Mexico City. Madero had not made any actual military plans to engage the Army of President Diaz (Federales). Since he had established a network of "non-reelection" committees throughout Mexico, perhaps he assumed the network system would provide him with a large army of volunteers. He knew he needed to create an insurgency to convince President Diaz to vacate the Presidency.

As matters turned out, Madero was obligated to enter into major combat operations when Pancho Villa and Pascual Orozco forced his hand in capturing Ciudad Juarez, a strategic city located along the U.S. border. Ciudad Juarez was an important city because it generated importation and exportation revenues, and it was the gateway for the shipment of arms and munitions into Mexico from the U.S.

In 1910, at the age of 32, Villa came to the attention of Abraham Gonzalez, a supporter of Madero and the former governor of the State of Chihuahua. Gonzalez, who was educated at Notre Dame, was an ex-banker and buyer of cattle who did not ask too many questions about the true ownership of the cattle being sold. Gonzalez requested to a meeting with Villa to explain to him the reasons that Madero had called for a Revolution against the Diaz Presidency. Gonzalez was well aware of Pancho Villa's reputation as a cattle thief and wide experience as a guerilla fighter.

When Villa and his bandit group went to visit Gonzalez, Villa did not trust him because he thought it was ploy or a setup by Gonzalez to capture him. Villa had to talk it over with his bandit group before they agreed to join the Revolution. Besides the high ideals of the Revolution, the bandit group was swayed by the fact they would be pardoned for their past criminal behavior. Also, they were delighted to learn that they could now confiscate property as lawful representatives of the government.

Until he met Abraham Gonzalez, Villa had never met a successful and educated person who would talk to him, person to person of such high ideals. He was impressed with the words used by Gonzalez to explain the aims of the Revolution and why Villa was needed to fight on behalf of the oppressed campesinos. A few weeks after meeting Gonzalez, Villa met Madero at the Hacienda Bustillos near Chihuahua City. Once again, Villa was impressed with Madero's plan for education, social justice, and land reform. Villa was in disbelief that Madero, a member of one of the wealthiest families in Mexico and was educated at the University of California, Berkeley, was willing to fight the Diaz regime to improve the lives of the campesinos. It seemed to Villa that this was an opportunity of a lifetime to correct the many years of injustices against the poor and disenfranchised that he had personally experienced since he was 16 years old. From this point on, Villa swore his unending loyalty and devotion to Madero and Gonzalez, and he became one of Madero's most trusted allies.

Acting on behalf of Francisco Madero, González commissioned Villa as a Captain in the Liberating Army of Madero, and ordered him to report to Colonel Castulo Herrera. Captain Villa and Colonel Herrera would fall under the overall command of General Pascual Orozco, who was preparing to attack the town of San Andres, Chihuahua. Since no funds were available, each commander was required to provide his own militia, including horses, rifles, and supplies. Villa started out with 15 Villistas, all members of his original bandolero group. He told each member of the group to recruit at least 10 men and bring them to San Andres. By the time Villa reported to Colonel Herrera, he had an army of over 300 soldiers, which almost doubled the size of Madero's army.

The first few days of the Revolution involved a number of small skirmishes where Villa was defeated by the better trained Federal troops. In November, Villa led a successful attack on San Andres, but the town was retaken a few days later when the Federales mounted a counter offensive. In December, he attacked a Federal stronghold at Cerro Gordo, near Chihuahua City, but here he was routed by the superior artillery of the Federales. In February 11, 1911, Villa attacked Ciudad Camargo, but with the arrival of Federal reinforcements, Villa had to retreat. Villa soon realized that the surprise attacks that he had conducted in the past, against unsuspecting victims when he was a bandolero, would not work against an army trained in military tactics. Villa, however, was quick to learn military protocols and soon taught his men how to obey military commands, deploy for an attack against a fortified position, use camouflage to conceal troop movements before an attack, and how to react against a counter offensive.

After losing several skirmishes, Villa and Coronel Orozco decided it would be necessary to take control of the extensive railroad system in the State of Chihuahua, if they were to succeed in defeating the Federal Army of President Diaz. The railroads would provide them with rapid deployment of their cavalry by transporting their supplies and the support of the Soldaderas, the Quartermaster Corps of the Revolution (at this time Villa and Orozco did not have any artillery). In the next few days, as the army of Orozco and Villa gained in numbers and strength, they took the towns of Pilar de Conchos and Estacion Bauche. Soon preparations were being made for the first major battle of the Revolution, the taking of Ciudad Juarez, a large city across the border from El Paso, Texas, and the pipeline for supplies and ammunition for the Revolution.

The battle for Ciudad Juarez was delayed for several days because Madero met with the Federal General Juan Medina to convince him to surrender the city. Villa and Orozco were frustrated by the delays and on their own initiative started the battle of Ciudad Juarez. Villa and Orozco were certain that once the battle was started, Madero would not be able to stop the military action. Madero tried in vain to stop the battle, but he was unable to find Villa and Orozco to order the cease fire. The battle for Ciudad Juarez lasted three days, from May 7 to May 10, 1911. The troops of Madero decisively defeated Federal General Juan Medina, who surrendered his forces on May 10. Most of the credit for the victory at Ciudad Juarez went to Villa for his outstanding leadership, the use of hand grenades, and his bravery in destroying established machine gun positions. Without a doubt, at Ciudad Juarez, Villa proved he was the master of guerilla tactical warfare. The defeat at Ciudad Juarez convinced Diaz that his time as the Dictator of Mexico was over. Hostilities ended with the signing of the Treaty of Juarez on May 25, 1911. President Diaz, escorted by General Huerta to the Port of Veracruz, left Mexico on the German ship *Ypiranga* to live in Paris, France, where he died on July 3, 1915.

The Revolution continues for nine more years

After the departure of President Diaz, the nation believed it had rid itself of dictators and had ushered in a new form of democratic government. But this was not the case because dictatorship breeds dictatorship and there were several generals loyal to President Diaz who wanted to continue with the Diaz regime. The Madero Presidency would last only 15 months before he was assassinated by a number of conspirators under the leadership of General Huerta.

As soon as Madero was assassinated, General Huerta coerced the Mexican Congress to appoint him as the President of Mexico. The forced Presidency by General Huerta was immediately challenged by Venustiano Carranza, the former Governor of the State of Coahuila. In the military campaigns to remove General Huerta from the Presidency, Pancho Villa, Emiliano Zapata, and Venustiano Carranza were at first united, but later became bitter enemies and would fight the bloodiest battles of the Revolution to decide the leadership of Mexico. For the next nine years, Pancho Villa would be in the thick of the Revolution, fighting tyrants who sought to control Mexico. Villa fought relentlessly for the ideals of Madero and Abraham Gonzalez until he retired from the Revolution in 1920, when he was given amnesty and a ranch by the Mexican Government.

Chapter VI.   Zapata and the Mexican Revolution

The two great legends of the Revolution, Pancho Villa and Emiliano Zapata, met, person to person, twice during the Mexican Revolution of 1910, and each time they met it was a historical event in the annals of the Revolution. They first met in June 1911 when they arrived in Mexico City to celebrate their victory over President Diaz; in June 1914; they met again in Mexico City to celebrate their victory over General Victoriano Huerta. Although they only met twice, when they met they embraced and admired each other. Many people assume that Villa and Zapata fought side by side in the same army during the Revolution. This was not the case because Zapata was in command of his own army in the south of Mexico, called the Liberating Army of the South, whereas Villa operated in the north of Mexico, where he commanded La Gran Division del Norte.

The Zapata family had lived in the village of Anenecuilco in the State of Morelos on land that was granted to them in the days of the Spanish Conquest. His people lived in "Pueblos" surrounded by small plots of farmland that they referred to as their Ancestral Lands. Zapata gained a reputation for training fine horses, owning his own home, and making a good living by growing watermelons. He also owned a mule train that he used to transport corn for the villagers for a fee and later carried bricks for local merchants. His economic status was perhaps one level above the campesinos that toiled the land. His parents were Gabriel Zapata and Cleofas Salazar. He came from a family of ten, but only four siblings survived: Epufemio, an older brother by five years, and two sisters, María de Jesus and María de Luz. His parents passed away one year apart when he was sixteen years of age.

Zapata, who was about 5' 6" in stature, was highly respected in his village. He was noted for having a huge mustache throughout his adult life and wearing fancy outfits when attending the village fiestas. To some it appeared he dressed like the hated Hacendados, but his people knew his heart belonged to the campesinos. In his early life he had two children with a very young woman, Inez Alfaro. His association with Inez Alfaro landed him trouble with the law, and he was forced to join the Mexican Army. He left the army within a few months, most likely because he paid someone in authority to obtain an early release. Zapata had some basic schooling, but he knew he needed to improve his education, so he became friends with Julio Torres Burgos, a local teacher, who helped him improve his reading and writing.

Zapata is elected to represent the villagers

The State of Morelos main industry was processing sugar from large sugar cane plantations owned by the Hacendados. Many of the plantations were owned by the hated Gachupines (native born Spaniards) or by absentee landlords. In the 1900's, the Hacendados were having difficulty generating profits from the sugar cane fields due to low production. Instead of investing in machinery to increase productivity, they found it expedient to absorb the ancestral lands owned by the campesinos. To acquire the land they coveted, they would cut off the water supply or file a false deed of trust, knowing that the campesinos did not have the money or the connections with the regime of President Diaz to fight the Hacendados in court. Eventually, many campesinos lost their land and had to go to work for the Hacendados as sharecroppers. Their wages were meager, and they were required to make all their purchases from La Tienda de Raya, the company store, at inflated prices or tricky arithmetic. This was a form of peonage, because the sharecroppers never made enough money to pay the Hacendados for seed, food, and cash advances, and each year they would become more heavily indebted. The debt was never paid off because it was passed on from generation to generation. Moreover, the sharecroppers could not escape this feudal system because if they did escape, they would be hunted by the infamous Rurales, a federal police force under the administration of President Diaz. The Rurales were notoriously known for applying La Ley Fuga, which meant that the suspect was shot while trying to escape.

In 1908, the Anenecuilco City Council commissioned Zapata to negotiate with the Diaz Government and the Hacendados for the return of their ancestral lands. Zapata's efforts were stymied when the Hacendados used their wealth and government power to stop Zapata. They had him incarcerated, placed in the Mexican Army for one year, and later sent to the Yucatan Peninsula to work as a laborer in the hemp fields.

When Zapata returned to Anenecuilco in 1909 he was elected Village Chief. He was now more determined than ever to regain the ancestral lands belonging to his village. Zapata was aware that challenging the large land barons would involve a legal fight in establishing their rights to regain their land. To prepare himself for the legal challenge ahead, he had the villagers pay for an attorney who went to Mexico City to research the legal title for their lands. Zapata and his close friend Francisco Franco spent eight days reading the documents obtained by the attorney. It required eight days to learn the value of the documents because the documents were written in the villagers' native Nahuatl language (Zapata spoke the native Nahuatl language).

Once Zapata was convinced that their lands had been stolen, he committed himself to doing whatever was necessary to restore their lands to the rightful owners. Before he confronted the local government for the return of their lands, Zapata buried the documents in a tin container in the mountains, just to make sure that someone else would be able to carry on in case he did not survive. When it became known that Zapata had buried the documents to safeguard them, many persons were impressed with his high ideals and total commitment to land reform.

In 1909, when the government refused to listen to Zapata's pleading for the return of their lands, he took matters into his own hands. He took eighty men to the local Hacienda and told the men working on the Hacienda to go home because the land they were cultivating did not belong to the Hacendado; it belonged to the villagers. This act of bravery would have sent the Rurales after him, but at this time President Diaz had bigger problems with the resurgence of Francisco Madero's 1910 campaign to become the President of Mexico.

By the time Zapata decided to join the Revolution with Madero to remove President Diaz, he had already been active in his home state of Morelos since 1908, pursuing the return of ancestral lands. Zapata was attracted to the Revolution because Madero's Plan de San Luis Potosi included a plank regarding agrarian reform and the proper distribution of confiscated land.

By June 1911, President Diaz had been defeated by the forces of Zapata, Villa, and Pascual Orozco. However, once Madero assumed the Presidency, Zapata quickly learned that Madero was not very politically astute. When Zapata went to visit Madero in Mexico City to discuss land reform, he made it very clear to Madero that the ancestral lands should be returned as soon as possible. Madero was hesitant and instead of being responsive, he informed Zapata that land reform required new legislation and this would take a considerable amount of time. In the meantime, Madero requested Zapata lay down his arms, which Zapata agreed to do. Unfortunately, while Zapata was instructing his rebel army to lay down their arms, Madero was maneuvered by Provisional President Francisco de la Barra, former ambassador to the United States under President Diaz, to conduct a military campaign of pacification against Zapata. De la Barra assigned the task to General Huerta, a ruthless general who took few prisoners. For the next few months, while Madero was attempting to seek reconciliation with Zapata, General Huerta was active pursuing Zapata to arrest or execute him. When Madero found out that General Huerta was being vindictive by burning villages, killing women and children and executing prisoners, he had him removed from his command. But it was too late, because Zapata had been misled too many times by Madero. Each time that Zapata was told that peace was at hand, Huerta would continue conducting military operations with the intent of destroying Zapata. Eventually, Zapata gave up on Madero and declared that he was in open rebellion against Madero and, under the *Plan de Ayala*, he would now fight until the villagers regained their ancestral lands.

The *Plan de Ayala* had two objectives: the rejection of Madero's Presidency, and, more importantly, Zapata wanted the land confiscated by the Hacendados be returned to the Pueblos. The Pueblos were townships made up of villagers who owned the land and only they could decide who would work the land, including what to grow, water rights, and the price for corn and vegetables. Under the regime of President Diaz, the Hacendado increased the number of haciendas from 5,000 to 9,000, by manipulating the law against the campesinos. They would file frivolous lawsuits contesting legal ownership and cut-off their water supply.

Assassination of General Emiliano Zapata

In 1919, President Carranza ordered General Pablo Gonzalez to invade the State of Morelos, Zapata's stronghold. Although General Gonzalez won several skirmishes against Zapata in the towns of Cuernavaca, Tetecala, Yautepec, and Jojutla, he was never able capture the elusive guerrilla fighter. Unable to capture Zapata in the field of battle, General Gonzalez then came up with a devious plan to trap Zapata. Colonel Jesus Guajardo, under the command of General Gonzalez, was found to have disobeyed orders when it was reported he was in a cantina instead of chasing Zapata. General Gonzalez did not incarcerate Guajardo but did place him under close surveillance by his commander. When Zapata learned that Guajardo was in trouble with General Gonzalez, he sent him a secret message asking Guajardo to join forces with him. Unknown to Zapata, the secret note was intercepted by Gonzalez, who reported the incident to Carranza. General Gonzalez then initiated a plan to let it be known that Guajardo wanted to cross over to the Zapata camp, an activity that occurred often during the Revolution.

Since Zapata was not sure of Guajardo's loyalty, he put him to a test. Zapata ordered Guajardo to take the village of Jonacatepec and capture Victoriano Barcenas, who had at one time betrayed Zapata. To demonstrate his loyalty, Guajardo took the village, but instead of capturing Barcenas, he had him executed.

Zapata seemed to be convinced of Guajardo's loyalty and agreed to meet with him to arrange for his troops to be incorporated into Zapata's army. They agreed to meet at the Hacienda Chinemeca, 15 miles from the town of Cuautla. Zapata was cautioned by his confidants that Guajardo's offer might be a trap. Nonetheless, accompanied by ten escorts, Zapata agreed to meet Guajardo. When Zapata arrived at the appointed hour he was hesitant to enter the Hacienda Chinemeca. Guajardo told Zapata everything was fine and that he should enter the Hacienda to enjoy some fine food and a beer. Guajardo also mentioned that he had assembled an Honor Guard to receive Zapata with appropriate military honors. The Honor Guard was a ruse to entice Zapata to enter the Hacienda grounds. As soon as the bugler was done with his salute for Zapata, Guajardo's troops fired two volleys. Zapata and his escorts were killed instantly. His body was first taken to General Gonzalez and later moved to the town square of Cuautla to be on display for the peasants to see for themselves that the immortal Zapata was now dead. Colonel Guajardo was promoted to General and the 50,000 pesos reward he received he distributed with the "Honor Guard" that assassinated Zapata.

On April 10, 1919, when Emiliano Zapata was assassinated in cold blood, he was 39 years old

The death of Zapata did not bring the Zapatista movement to an end. His dedication to agrarian reform was adopted by the nation as the standard for improving the lives of the campesinos. Zapata did not die in vain. Since his death, every succeeding President of Mexico made it a point to pursue legislation for the proper return of ancestral lands that Zapata had given his life for. In modern times, the name Zapata continues to resonate with the downtrodden and disenfranchised, such as the Zapatistas in the State of Chiapas. Several recent social movements have adopted his name to symbolize his motto, *"Prefiero morir de pie que vivir de rodillas."* ("It is better to die upon your feet than to live upon your knees!") Zapata and Villa, the two icons of the Revolution stayed true to their ideals and neither became rich from the spoils of war.

Chapter VII.   The Revolt of General Pascual Orozco

General Orozco and Pancho Villa had served Madero well in bringing about the removal of Porfirio Diaz as the dictator of Mexico. When the Revolution ended, Villa retired to private life with the rank of Colonel. Pascual Orozco believed he was entitled to serve as Minister of War. However, the post was given to General Venustiano Carranza, and Orozco was designated the Military Commander of the State of Chihuahua, and this disappointed him. By December 1911, with the financial support of dissident land barons, Orozco was in rebellion against the Madero Administration. When Madero learned of Orozco's association with the Hacendados, he asked that Villa monitor the political activities of Orozco and the Hacendados in Chihuahua.

During the campaign to defeat Orozco, Huerta demonstrated his dislike of Villa. Huerta was an old line general from the Diaz regime who expected military obedience and total subordination regarding military orders. Villa did not comport with the image that Huerta expected of a general. Villa operated as a maverick general who won decisive battles by employing guerilla warfare tactics and did not always adhere to military protocols. In addition, Villa was gaining a larger-than-life reputation because he was winning battles for the Revolution, and Huerta felt he was losing the center stage as the overall commander of the campaign to defeat Orozco.

Villa Sent to Prison by General Huerta

In the Battle of Rellano near Jimenez, Chihuahua, Villa confiscated a beautiful Arabian horse from one of the Hacendados, an incident that almost cost him his life. Huerta ordered Villa to return the horse immediately to its rightful owner. Villa was unable to respond because he was bedridden with the flu. Since Huerta harbored animosity towards Villa, he deemed Villa's failure to return the horse a failure to obey military orders. General Huerta ordered that Villa be arrested for disobeying orders, and added the bogus charge that Villa had stolen money from the citizens of Parral, Chihuahua. Villa was placed in jail in the City of Parral and later moved to a military prison in Chihuahua City for immediate execution before a firing squad. Many attempts were made by the supporters of Villa to spare his life. Eventually, Emilio and Raul Madero, brothers of President Madero, intervened to obtain a stay of execution. President Madero ordered that Villa be sent to Military Prison in Mexico City.

The order by President Madero to stop the execution of Villa was viewed by Huerta as another instance of interfering in military matters. When Huerta was given command, he was assured that President Madero would not interfere in military matters. It also happens that the reprieve given to Villa was the second time that President Madero rebuffed General Huerta. In 1911, General Huerta was ordered to undertake a campaign to pacify Zapata in the State of Morelos. General Huerta was relieved of his command when President Madero learned that General Huerta was using excessive force to destroy Zapata, rather than pursue pacification methods.

Villa was sent to prison at Santiago Tlatelolco in Mexico City where he was placed in solitary confinement for three months.

While in prison, Villa was befriended by Carlos Jauregui, a court clerk who believed that Villa had been wrongfully imprisoned. Jauregui became a confidant who taught Villa how to read and write. Not all historians agree on this point. Some suggest Villa was taught by the intellectual Flores Magon, a supporter of Zapata who was also in prison. While in prison, Villa learned from reliable informants that Huerta and several other conspirators were planning to revolt against the Madero administration.

Villa Escapes to El Paso, Texas

With the aid of Jauregui and his brother Hipolito, Villa escaped from prison on December 27, 1912, disguised as an attorney in civilian clothes with a top hat. He travelled along the Mexican Pacific coast hiding in the cities of Nayarit, Mazatlan, and Guaymas, Sonora until he arrived at El Paso, Texas, on January 2, 1913. In El Paso, Villa held meetings with Madero supporters in an effort to warn Madero about Huerta's plan to overthrow his administration.

Unfortunately, Madero truly believed that his diplomatic skills were sufficient to keep the plotters in check. Villa, being more certain of his instincts and of Huerta's intentions, began to plan his return to Mexico in the event of an overthrow by Huerta. Villa's misgivings about Huerta were soon realized when Villa learned that Madero and Vice President Pino Suárez had been assassinated on February 22, 1913. Later he also learned that his good friend Abraham Gonzalez, the former governor of the State of Chihuahua and the person who convinced Villa to join the Revolution, had been assassinated near the City of Chihuahua on March 7, 1913. Gonzalez's body had been placed on rails and run over by a train. Gonzalez was assassinated by order of Huerta

81

because Gonzalez was an ally of Madero and one of the principal movers to join Madero in the Revolution to remove President Diaz from the Presidency.

The deaths of Madero and Gonzalez deeply infuriated Villa because they were the two most important individuals who introduced Villa to the Revolution. Villa felt that Madero and Gonzalez had given him a once-in-a-lifetime opportunity to fight against injustice and the oppression of the disenfranchised, and now he would seek revenge against Huerta. He viewed Huerta as a drunkard and treacherous person who needed to be brought to justice for the Cuartelazo (overthrow) he committed against Madero and Pino Suárez.

To return to Chihuahua, Villa needed funds to buy munitions, horses, and provisions, so he borrowed 3,000 pesos from his brother Hipolito. He had earlier received 1,500 pesos from Abraham Gonzalez and a lesser amount from José María Maytorena, Governor of the State of Sonora. With provisions consisting of coffee, sugar, and salt, Villa, along with Jauregui and six other men, crossed the border into Mexico at Ysleta, Texas, on March 13, 1913. Villa was on his way to Satevo in the State of Chihuahua, to avenge the death of his beloved idols, Francisco Madero and Abraham Gonzalez.

Chapter VIII. Assassination of President Madero

President Francisco Madero and his Vice President, Pino Suárez, were assassinated on February 22, 1913. Mexican historians commonly refer to the Madero and Pino Suárez assassination as La Decena Tragica, or "Ten Tragic Days" from February 9 to February 19, 1913. The assassination involved the highest level of government treason, intrigue, betrayal, and foreign intervention by a number of conspirators who wished to return to the ways of the Porfirio Diaz regime, the Porfirato Period.

Several conspirators were involved in the assassination: General Victoriano Huerta, who at the time of the revolt was on military leave in Mexico City recuperating from an eye infection; General Felix Diaz, nephew of exiled President Diaz, who was in the military prison in Mexico City for trying to take military control of the State of Veracruz; General Bernardo Reyes, a one-time candidate for the Presidency against Madero, in a civilian prison in Mexico City for leading a revolt in the State of Nuevo Leon; General Manuel Mondragón, a Diaz loyalist; General Aureliano Blanquet, in charge of the garrison at the National Palace; Colonel Francisco Cardenas, Commander of the Rurales; and U.S. Ambassador Henry Lane Wilson, who covertly participated in the overthrow of President Madero.

On June 10, 1910, after defeating the army of Porfirio Diaz, Madero rode his horse triumphantly into Mexico City as the foremost hero of the Revolution. He was received by cheering crowds shouting *Viva Madero*. When Madero officially assumed the Presidency in December 1911, the nation believed the days of tyrants and dictators had come to an end. Madero was the first President elected to office in thirty years by a true electoral process that was free of ballot stuffing, voter fraud, and voter intimidation. However, the hopes for an enlightened democracy were quickly dashed when it was realized that Madero was an eternal optimist and not a politically astute administrator.

Madero made a number of critical mistakes that contributed to his downfall: he failed to assume the Presidency as soon as Diaz was removed; he failed to remove a number of legislators that owed their allegiance to Diaz; he permitted many of his adversaries to plot against his Presidency; he permitted newspapers and journalists to attack his administration without providing a proper rebuttal; he failed to reach an accord with Emiliano Zapata; and he vested excessive military power in General Victoriano Huerta. Most importantly, he failed to adequately assess the intentions of U.S. Ambassador Henry Lane Wilson to destroy his Presidency.

Madero's Presidency lasted only fifteen months. The aftermath caused by the assassination of Madero set in motion a Revolution that lasted from 1913 to 1920. When Madero assumed the Presidency in 1911, no one could foresee that General Victoriano Huerta would conspire to assassinate him, or that General Francisco "Pancho" Villa would engage General Venustiano Carranza in the bloodiest battles of the Revolution to determine the leadership of Mexico.

Madero Fails to Take Firm Control

In May 1911, Madero's revolutionary force soundly defeated the Federal army of Porfirio Diaz in the Battle of Ciudad Juarez. Madero's victory led to the Treaty of Ciudad Juarez, ending all hostilities between Madero and Diaz. However, according to the

Plan de San Luis Potosi issued by Madero on November 20, 1910, Madero was to become the Provisional President as soon as Diaz was removed. Since Diaz resigned in June 1911, Madero should have assumed the Provisional Presidency then and there. However, as a compromise for Diaz leaving Mexico immediately, Madero agreed that Francisco de la Barra would serve as Interim President for the last six months of the Diaz Presidency. The ever optimistic Madero wanted to wait six months to assume the reins of government, until the formal elections in December. Madero wanted to be in compliance with the Constitution of Mexico for the new President to assume office in December.

Madero believed this step was necessary to preserve the integrity of a true and free electoral process. This was an unwise decision on the part of Madero because it gave Mexico two heads of state, a situation that caused confusion in authority, particularly in view of the need to checkmate a large number of Diaz loyalists still in power. It also denied Madero the initiative to forcefully assume leadership and gain full control of the nation. De la Barra, who had served as Foreign Minister to the U.S. under Diaz, was still beholden to the Diaz regime.

From a political perspective, Madero's biggest mistake was his inability to reach an accord with the demands by Zapata for the immediate return of ancestral lands to the indigenous campesinos in the State of Morelos. Instead of being responsive to Zapata, and believing in the true virtues of democracy, he asked that Zapata lay down his arms and deactivate his army. Zapata considered Madero's response an insult to the aims of the Revolution.

Before joining the Revolution, Zapata had met with Madero's representatives and made it clear that he wanted land reform accepted as a condition of joining the Revolution. Matters became more complicated when de la Barra, with the concurrence of Madero, initiated an ill-advised military campaign to disarm Zapata. The campaign was assigned to General Victoriano Huerta, an old general known for treating his prisoners with brutality while under the Diaz regime.

Since Madero wanted reconciliation with Zapata and Huerta wanted imprisonment, there was a falling out between Madero and Huerta. Eventually Madero convinced de la Barra to relieve Huerta from his command. Removing General Huerta would have serious repercussions for Madero the following year when General Huerta led a revolt against President Madero.

In addition to the military campaign against Zapata, Madero completely underestimated the inflammatory actions of U.S. Ambassador Henry Lane Wilson, who was an outspoken critic of the Madero Presidency. Ambassador Wilson, a leftover of President Taft's "Dollar Diplomacy" Administration, began to send messages to Washington that Madero was not fit to be President of Mexico. Ambassador Wilson did not believe that Madero would grant American business interests the same protection and profits provided under the Diaz dynasty.

Ambassador Wilson participated with Huerta, Felix Diaz, Bernardo Reyes, and the other conspirators by attending clandestine meetings where plans were being made to remove Madero from the Presidency. He sent untruthful communiqués to President Wilson stating that Madero was incompetent, that he was disliked by foreign representatives, and that Madero did not have the support of the nation's constituency.

The Ten Tragic Days

The timeline during which President Madero and Vice-President Suarez were removed from office and later assassinated is known in Mexico as the "Decena Tragica" or The Ten Tragic Days. The assassination came about when several high level Mexican generals and U.S. Ambassador Henry Lane Wilson had a meeting of the minds that President Madero and his Vice-President had to resign or be removed from office by force. The Decena Tragica, February 9 to February 19, 1913, involved ten days of intrigue and betrayal of the highest order against a freely elected President. The treacherous act of military officers Victoriano Huerta, Felix Diaz, Bernardo Reyes, Manuel Mondragon, Aureliano Blanquet, Gregorio Ruiz, Francisco Cardenas, and U.S. Ambassador Henry Lane Wilson shall forever be negatively associated with the history of Mexico.

The conspirators involved military officers that remained in office because President Madero had failed to purge the federal army of officers still loyal to deposed President Diaz. Henry Lane Wilson had been appointed Ambassador to Mexico in 1910, under Republican President Howard Taft (Ambassador Wilson was a lame-duck appointee who would soon be replaced by President Woodrow Wilson, a Democrat who had just been elected, but would not assume the presidency until, March 4, 1913).

General Huerta, who was on inactive military status, was in Mexico City to receive medical attention for his eyesight. In the previous two years, Huerta had had confrontations with President Madero on two occasions. In October 1912, Huerta was removed from command by President Madero because he was conducting an aggressive military campaign to imprison and execute Emiliano Zapata in the State of Morelos. His military orders were to capture Zapata and conduct a pacification program. Contrary to his orders, Huerta was conducting a campaign of death and destruction. In 1911, President Madero assigned Huerta to repel the revolt of General Pascual Orozco in the State of Chihuahua. To

87

defeat Orozco, General Francisco "Pancho" Villa was promoted to Brigadier General by President Madero, and made subordinate to Huerta. During the campaign against Orozco, Huerta, who resented the military independence of Villa, ordered that he be arrested and executed by a firing squad. Villa was accused of stealing a fine horse from a prominent hacendado, as well as having misused some monies from the municipality of Parral, Chihuahua. President Madero intervened in the execution and ordered that Villa be sent to prison in Mexico City, a decision that infuriated General Huerta. General Felix Diaz was in a civilian prison in Mexico City because he had led a revolt against President Madero in the State of Veracruz. General Reyes was in the Mexico City military prison because he had led a short lived revolt against President Madero in the State of Nuevo Leon. General Mondragon was an old line general who had gained a fortune by manipulating military purchase orders for munitions while serving under President Diaz and was determined to return to the former Porfirato Period. General Blanquet was in the nearby City of Toluca, in charge of 1,200 federal troops. General Gregorio Ruiz was the Minister of War, and Major Francisco Cardenas was the Commander of Rurales in Mexico City.

The conspirator's initial plan was for Reyes to become Provisional President, and at a later date Reyes would support Felix Diaz, nephew of former President Diaz, to be formally elected President of Mexico. Shortly before the revolt was initiated, a list of twenty-two names, including the name of Huerta, was received by Gustavo Madero (brother of President Madero). Although President Madero was properly forewarned when he received the list of mutineers, President Madero did not believe that Huerta and the other conspirators were capable of an insurrection. The revolt started in the early hours of Sunday,

February 9, when the conspirators went to the civilian prison to free Felix Diaz, and then to the military prison to free Bernardo Reyes. At first, the group was led by General Mondragon who was able to convince the military cadets at the Cavalry School to join the revolt. In total, the rebels consisted of some 1,400 insurrectionists, 300 military cadets, 300 cavalry troops, 400 soldiers, to be joined by 400 National Palace Guards, who had agreed to turn against President Madero. The insurrection was underway as soon as Diaz and Reyes were released from prison. General Diaz departed for the local armory (La Ciudadela) located about two miles from the National Palace to capture arms and munitions. General Reyes was assigned to capture the National Palace and force the resignation of President Madero.

The overall events involved in the revolt are difficult to follow because of the many changes in direction that took place on a daily basis during the ten day period. Moreover, the authors believe the "cuartelazo" (coup d'état) could not have succeeded without the explicit participation of U.S. Ambassador Henry Lane Wilson. Therefore from a historical perspective, it is critical to clarify the role played by the main conspirators in the removal and assassination of President Madero and Vice-President Pino Suarez.

A recounting of the main events is perhaps the best approach to assist the reader understand how the insurrection was initiated, changed course during the rebellion, and culminated in the assassination of President Madero and Vice-President Pino Suarez.

February 9

- The insurrectionists arrive at the civilian prison to release Felix Diaz, and then move to the military prison to free Bernardo Reyes. Felix Diaz marches to the

Ciudadela, the local armory, to capture arms and munitions. Reyes marches to the National Palace to force the resignation of President Madero. The military cadets, led by Col. Juan Morales, arrived first at the National Palace. They were met by Gustavo Madero, brother of President Madero, who is able to convince the cadets to withdraw because they were about to commit treason against the President of Mexico. General Lauro Villar, Commander of the National Palace, is alerted that the insurrectionists will return later that morning. When Reyes arrives with an armed militia, he is met with a fusillade by General Villar. Reyes is killed instantly, and General Villar is mortally wounded. General Gregorio Ruiz surrenders and is immediately executed for treason. The insurrection is temporarily halted, and the insurrectionists retreat to regroup at the Ciudadela, commandeered by Diaz.

- Huerta is at the side of President Madero when the attack takes place at the National Palace. Huerta has knowledge of the conspiracy to overthrow President Madero, but as yet, he was not one of the main conspirators. With General Villar near death, President Madero was concerned as to who would defend the National Palace. At that moment, Huerta stated to President Madero, "I know of only one person who could take your troops and stop this damned rebellion." When asked whom would that person be, Huerta responded by saying, "With the proper authority, I'm the person to quash the rebellion." At this moment, President remembered that it was Huerta who had put down the rebellion of Pascual Orozco in the State of Chihuahua. President Madero was skeptical about Huerta, but since there was no other experienced general available, he accepted the services of Huerta and designated him as the Commander of for the Defense of Mexico City.

- When Gustavo Madero learned that Huerta had been placed in charge, he had him arrested because he did not trust Huerta. When President Madero found out about the arrest, he had him released and admonished his brother Gustavo for distrusting Huerta. President Madero still believed that he would be properly protected by Huerta. Unfortunately for Gustavo, his interference would later cost him his life.

- President Madero leaves Mexico City to confer with General Felipe Angeles at nearby Cuernavaca, Morelos. (General Angeles had replaced Huerta in pursuing Zapata.) President Madero had such a high regard for General Angeles that only a few months earlier he had promoted him to Brigadier General.

February 10
- When President Madero arrives in Mexico City with Angeles and a contingent of 1,000 federal troops, he faces a setback when he is informed that Angeles cannot assume command of the troops because his promotion to Brigadier General had not been approved by the Congress. Consequently, Angeles is placed as second in command under Huerta. This reversal will have serious consequences for President Madero and Vice-President Pino Suarez, as well as Angeles.

- President Madero sends a telegram to General Aureliano Blanquet in the City of Toluca, fifty miles from Mexico City, to prepare a forced march to Mexico City. Blanquet is to arrive as soon as possible with 1,200 troops to defend the National Palace.

February 11

- While the insurrection is underway, Ambassador Wilson exaggerates reports to President Taft by stating that the nation was out of control, that General Zapata's Army was on its way to invade Mexico City, and that measures are needed to be taken to stop the destruction and bloodshed. All of these developments play precisely into the hands of Huerta who now believes he can control the outcome of the insurrection by meeting secretly with General Diaz and Ambassador Wilson. More importantly, Huerta is led to believe by Ambassador Wilson that if he assumes the Presidency, he will be recognized by President Taft.

- During the next days, Huerta continues to meet with the conspirators, while at the same time ordering several attacks on the Ciudadela without any intent of defeating the rebels. Moreover, he orderes troops loyal to President Madero to attack at certain strong points knowing they will be annihilated by the rebel forces. Angeles, as second in command, is in no position to second guess the motives and tactics of Huerta. As a result, hundreds of civilians are killed or wounded and considerable damage is inflicted on buildings during the ten day siege.

February 12

- Ambassador Wilson now takes the view that President Madero is responsible for the bloodshed because he refused to resign. To lend support to his position he confers with several Latin American countries, including the Austrian and Japanese legations, to obtain their approval to ask for the resignation of President Madero. The representatives of these foreign governments respond by advising Ambassador Wilson that President Madero had been democratically elected as President, and thus has the power and authority to bring the rebellion under control. In addition, they stated that foreign diplomats have no business interfering in the internal affairs of President's Madero administration.

- The Ambassador next calls on the ministers from Britain, Germany, and Spain to inform them that President Madero should resign. Ambassador Wilson has no further contact with the Latin American countries on the basis that the British, German, and Spanish governments represent the "greatest interest, and the others really didn't matter."

February 13

- Ambassador Wilson visits Pedro Lascurain, President Madero's Foreign Minister, to make it clear that President Madero should resign. Ambassador Wilson informs Lascurain that President Madero's refusal to resign will be the direct cause of the bloodshed and destruction in Mexico City and the potential invasion of Mexico by the U. S. military.

- Ambassador Wilson continued to misinformed the U.S. State Department that Mexican public opinion and foreign dignitaries all believed that President Madero was responsible for the upheaval in Mexico City.

February 15

- Ambassador Wilson requests the British, German, and Spanish ministers come to a meeting at the U.S. Embassy to discuss the resignation of President Madero. The ministers agree that a resignation is in order and the Spanish minister is designated as the person to deliver the message. President Madero rejects the plea by the Spanish Minister. He indicates to the Spanish Minister that they have no authority to interfere in the internal affairs of Mexico, and further, a forced resignation would surely plunge Mexico into chaos and another revolution.

- Later in the day, Ambassador Wilson, accompanied by the German Minster, goes to the National Palace to confer with Huerta. When they arrive, they are taken to the office of President Madero where an armistice is arranged to take place on Sunday, February 16, to bury the dead and remove innocent by-standers from the combat zone.

February 16

- General Blanquet arrives with his regiment. He had taken five days to travel fifty miles and had no intention of defending President Madero.

- That evening, Ambassador Wilson sends a communiqué to the State Department stating he had received a secret message from Huerta, saying, "He expected to take steps tonight towards terminating the situation."

- The coup d'état did not take place that night as forecasted by Ambassador Wilson, and the next day Ambassador Wilson advises Secretary Knox that he had received another message from Huerta indicating that President Madero would soon be removed and the "plans were fully matured."

February 17
- Ambassador Wilson contacts newspaper reporters to inform them that President Madero would be arrested at noon on Tuesday, February 18.

February 18
- Ambassador Wilson makes contact with Pedro Lascurain, Minister of Foreign Relations, to convey to Congress that President Madero must resign. By not resigning, Ambassador Wilson asserts that President Madero is to blame for the bloodshed and destruction of Mexico City. When contacted by Lascurain, President Madero refuses to resign.

- When the reporters arrive on Tuesday to witness the resignation of President Madero, they are disappointed to find the insurrectionists had not arrived at noon at the National Palace as predicted by Ambassador Wilson.

- In the meantime, the shrewd Huerta invites Gustavo Madero to the Grambinas Restaurant for breakfast. Gustavo was not aware that the invitation was a clandestine move intended to remove him as an obstacle for the takeover of the government. As Gustavo was about to leave the restaurant, he was forcibly arrested and taken as a prisoner to the Ciudadela.

- As soon as Gustavo was imprisoned, Gen. Aureliano Blanquet leaves for the National Palace to arrest President Madero, Vice-President Pino Suarez, and General Angeles. When they arrive, Blanquet orders Lt. Col. Teodoro Jimenez Riverol and Major Izquierdo to arrest President Madero. With pistols in hand, President Madero is told he was under arrest. President Madero told Riverol he was traitor. As Riverol and Izquierdo are about to shoot President Madero, Riverol is killed by Capt. Gustavo Garmendia and Izquierdo is shot by Capt. Federico Montez. As the other insurrectionists try to shoot President Madero, an aide, Marcos Hernandez, steps forward and takes bullets meant for President Madero. As President Madero seeks to escape, he is captured by General Blanquet. President Madero, Pino Suarez, and General Angeles, are held as prisoners in the basement of the National Palace.

- By 2 PM that afternoon Ambassador Wilson sends a message to the U.S. State Department, "My confidential messenger with Huerta has just communicated to me Madero's arrest."

- Ambassador Wilson then takes action to call for a meeting that night at 9 PM between Huerta, Diaz, and himself at the American Embassy (The Embassy Pact). The conspirators spend three hours trying to arrive at a formal agreement on who would be the new leader of the nation, organizing a new government and cabinet, and what should be done with President Madero and Vice-President Pino Suarez. A plan for a new leader is necessary because General Bernardo Reyes, who was scheduled to be the new Provisional President, was killed on the first day of the revolt.

- During the Embassy Pact meeting, Huerta and Diaz argue who should be the Provisional President. Diaz claims he was the leader, and as the initiator of the revolt, he should be entitled to the Presidency. Huerta claims that when he turned on Madero, he in effect took control of the Federal army, and without him, the revolt could not have succeeded. On several occasions, as the meeting is about to fall apart, Ambassador Wilson keeps working with them towards a resolution. In the end they reach a compromise: Madero would be forced to resign the Presidency, and Huerta would become the Provisional President until elections could be held in October, at which time he would support Felix Diaz for the Presidency. They also agree that none of the ministers under Madero would be harmed and a new cabinet would be formed.

- That night, after the Embassy Pact was formally ratified by Huerta, Diaz, and Ambassador Wilson, Gustavo Madero is taken outside the Ciudadela to an empty lot, severely beaten and shot to death.

February 19
- On this day, while being held prisoners, President Madero and Vice-President Suarez resign under duress.

They were told that if they didn't resign, harm would come to Madero's wife and mother. President Madero agrees to resign when he was given assurances his family would not be harmed, members of his cabinet would not be executed, and some of the state governors he had appointed would be allowed to stay in office. President Madero also believes that, once in Cuba, he will be able to return to Mexico because the conspirators will not be able to hold on to an illegitimate presidency.

- The resignations were to be placed in the hands of the Chilean and Cuban Ministers until President Madero and Vice-President Suarez and their families were safely out of the country and on their way to Cuba. President Madero and Vice-President Suarez were to be removed from the federal prison and taken to the railroad station where they would be joined by their families, and the Chilean and Cuban ministers were to escort them to the Port of Veracruz. By late evening, President Madero and Vice-President Suarez had not yet arrived at the railroad station, so the Chilean Minister leaves to see Huerta about the delay. When he arrives, Huerta refuses to see him that night. It was reported that President Madero and Vice-President Suarez were not released because the plan was for the train to Veracuz to be blown-up, and this would no longer be possible because the Chilean and Cuban minister would be on the train.

February 20
- Since President Madero and Vice-President both resigned, according to the Mexican Constitution of 1857, the order of succession falls on the Attorney General,

(Adolfo Valles Baca), Minister of Foreign Relations (Pedro Lascurain), and Minister of Interior. Since President Madero, Vice-President Suarez, and Attorney General Baca had all resigned, Lascurain was now the President of Mexico. Lascurain then appointed Huerta as the Minister of Interior and within a few minutes Lascurain resigns as President. The process that was followed left a clear path for Huerta to ascend to the Presidency. All of this was quickly approved by Congress because Huerta had his military aides attend the proceedings armed with weapons.

February 21

- Early in the evening, Col. Luis Vallesteres arrives at the penitentiary to replace the Commandant of the prison.

- Near midnight, President Madero and Vice-President Suarez are taken from the National Palace in two automobiles and escorted to the federal prison by Major Francisco Cardenas.

February 22

- Near midnight, when they arrive at the prison, the two automobiles are parked at a vacant lot near the prison. The next day it was reported that President Madero and Vice-President Suarez were either assassinated by the escort under the command of Major Cardenas or they were killed by cross fire when they attempted to escape (La Ley Fuga).

- Although Huerta wants General Felipe Angeles executed, his life is spared because of his outstanding record in training cadets at the military academy, and

Huerta did not want to incur the wrath of cadets, as well as the many others who held Angeles in high regard. As a result, Angeles was charged with insubordination and sent to prison. A few months later, the charges are dropped when Huerta realizes that Angeles is held in high regard by many influential Mexicans as well as some leading foreigners.

Most of the nation and the Revolutionary leaders that ousted the former Dictator President Diaz quickly declared that they were against Huerta. Once again the Revolutionary leaders came together in an effort to remove another dictator from the Presidency. With both Madero and Pino Suárez eliminated, there was a need for new leadership. Venustiano Carranza took action to assume the title of Primer Jefe, or First Chief of the Constitution. Carranza initiated the Plan de Guadalupe, a manifesto in which he declared Huerta's Presidency null and void. Recently elected U.S. President Woodrow Wilson was taken aback by Huerta's betrayal, and, as a matter of American policy, declared that Huerta should be removed from the Presidency, by force, if necessary.

From a historical perspective, it is important to note that Huerta had Madero and Pino Suárez assassinated at the same time. Without a doubt, Huerta had calculated that it was necessary for both Madero and Pino Suárez to be removed simultaneously in order to create a vacuum for the Presidency, otherwise, if Pino Suárez had survived, he would have been entitled, according to the Constitution of Mexico, to assume the Presidency. Huerta certainly knew what he was doing insofar as removing all obstacles before taking control of the government of Mexico.

Another tragic outcome related to the assassination of Madero was the treatment accorded Mrs. Madero during the Ten Tragic Days. While Madero was being held in prison, Mrs. Madero visited Ambassador Wilson to plead for her husband's life. The Ambassador's response was that the U.S. does not interfere in the internal matters of a foreign country. Fearful for her life, Mrs. Madero sought refuge with the Ambassador from Japan. Eventually, Mrs. Madero was given safe passage to San Antonio, Texas.

The assassination of President Madero caused the Revolution to continue for seven more years, from 1913 to 1920. During the first months of military operations to remove Huerta, Carranza had the support of Villa and Zapata. However, as the military campaign unfolded, it became evident that Carranza's real ambition was to become the President of Mexico, at any cost. In the campaign to defeat Huerta, Carranza made a number of decisions intended to prevent Villa and Zapata from entering Mexico City first, and thus claim the leadership of Mexico. Villa and Zapata were well aware of Carranza's intentions to become President of México, but nonetheless they agreed to support the Revolution until the forces of Huerta were defeated.

Chapter IX.   General Felipe Ángeles

General Felipe Ángeles was perhaps the most intelligent, articulate and patriotic general of the Revolution. His tactical knowledge on the use of artillery, smokeless explosive powder, and machine guns as offensive weapons was recognized by military leaders all over the world. Although an outstanding military leader, he did not achieve the notoriety of Villa, Zapata, Obregon, and Carranza, for several reasons. Felipe Ángeles did not enter the Revolution as a revolutionary leader of a particular faction; did not expound on any manifestos on his ideals for the Revolution, and he did not demonstrate ambition to become the President of Mexico. He was simply a highly competent general who believed that Mexico should be rid of dictators and tyrants that professed to act in the best interest of Mexico, but actually coveted power and dictatorship.

Ángeles was born on June 13, 1868, in Zacualtipan, Hidalgo. He was the son of Colonel Felipe Ángeles, who had fought in the war against the United States in 1847, and in 1861, fought against the French occupation under Emperor Maximilian. The elder Colonel Ángeles and his wife Juana Ramirez had four children, Felipe, Cristina, Eduardo, and Leopoldo. General Ángeles attended primary schools in Molango, Hidalgo and the Instituto Literario in Pachuca. In 1883, at age fourteen, he entered the Military Academy in Mexico City where he excelled in mathematics. He was selected for entrance to the academy based on his intellect and high grades in mathematics, compared to other cadets who were allowed to attend the academy because they came from wealthy families. After graduating from the academy, Ángeles was steadily promoted until he reached the rank of full colonel, the same rank attained by his father. Due to his outstanding record in mathematics and engineering, he was asked to remain at the academy as an instructor to the cadets. While at the academy, he met and married Clara Kraus, a school teacher from California who, at the time, was teaching school in Mexico City. Felipe and Clara had four children: Alberto, Isabel, Felipe, and Julio.

From the beginning in his military career, Ángeles was able to demonstrate his competence and integrity. In 1902, Colonel Ángeles and General Manuel Mondragon were sent to France to purchase cannons for the Mexican Army. When the deal was completed, Mondragon asked the French government to add 25% of the cost of the invoice to cover his commission. Ángeles objected to the added cost and refused to sign the purchase order. In 1904, Ángeles was sent to the U.S. to purchase gun powder. He conducted several tests and determined that the proposed gun powder did not meet correct standards for artillery use. In 1906, Ángeles was confined to quarters for eight days because he had written a negative critique on the poor quality of the training provided to non-commissioned officers.

In 1908, Ángeles was sent to the French Military Academy in France to become an expert in the use of artillery. He was awarded the order of Knight of the Legion of Honor by the French Government for his outstanding contributions in researching ballistics, gun powder and the tactical use of artillery as an offensive weapon. When the revolution broke out in 1910 against President Porfirio Diaz, Ángeles was still in Paris and was unable to return to Mexico until 1912. When he returned to Mexico, he was appointed by President Madero as Superintendent of the Military Academy at Chapultepec Castle. Under Madero, Ángeles gained a reputation as a dignified officer and a person of honor, and in June 1912, he was nominated as Brigadier General.

Ángeles joins the Revolution

After the assassination of Madero, Huerta was unsure of what to do with Ángeles because Ángeles had many supporters in Mexico City, including U.S. Ambassador Henry Lane Wilson. First, he ordered that Ángeles be held in prison for six months. While in prison, Huerta ordered that Ángeles be court martialed for having killed a rebellious teenager during the revolt against Madero. The charges against Ángeles were suspended because they could not be proven, as well as the fact that many influential friends came to his aid. Since Huerta was intent on removing Ángeles, as a last resort, he had Ángeles exiled to Paris, France, on a military mission.

When Ángeles learned of the betrayal by General Huerta, he immediately left France to return to Mexico to offer his services to Primer Jefe Venustiano Carranza. At first, Ángeles was welcomed by Carranza and was appointed Secretary of War. However, within a few weeks Ángeles fell out of favor with General Alvaro Obregon, a confidant of Carranza. Obregon and some of the other generals of the revolution protested that Ángeles was a product of the military Dictatorship of Porfirio Diaz, and, moreover, he had not fought in the Revolution to remove President Diaz. (General Ángeles had been on military duty in France.)

The real reasons for disliking Ángeles were not clear. Perhaps Carranza and Obregon were jealous of Ángeles because he had several important attributes: superior military training, superior military mind, and was unwilling to be involved in corruption. Eventually, the animosity against Ángeles resulted in Ángeles being relegated to Sub-Secretary of War under General Alvaro Obregon. In spite of being demoted, it was Ángeles who planned a brilliant military campaign to remove Huerta. The plan developed by Ángeles was to create three field armies that would advance in unison on established railroad lines from the North of

105

Mexico to converge as one force in Mexico City. The army of General Alvaro Obregon would advance from the State of Sonora, the Army of General Pancho Villa would advance from the State of Chihuahua, and General Pablo Gonzalez would advance from the State of Coahuila. In addition, General Emiliano Zapata would apply pressure from the South, from the State of Morelos. The plan worked brilliantly and by July 1914, the forces of Huerta had been defeated.

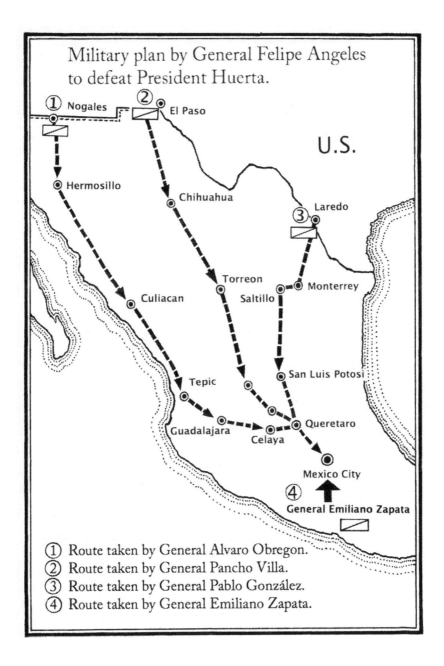

Military plan by General Felipe Angeles to defeat President Huerta.

① Route taken by General Alvaro Obregon.
② Route taken by General Pancho Villa.
③ Route taken by General Pablo González.
④ Route taken by General Emiliano Zapata.

Ángeles joins Pancho Villa

After being demoted to Sub-Secretary of War, Ángeles was not happy in Mexico City under Carranza and Obregon. In January 1914, Carranza and Ángeles made a trip to visit Villa in Chihuahua City. Ángeles immediately sensed that he would rather serve under Villa. He convinced Villa to ask Carranza that he be transferred. In March 1914, Ángeles joined Villa as the Artillery Officer for the Division of the North.

Ángeles became Villa's main military adviser and confidant. His expert knowledge of artillery enabled Villa to win some of the greatest battles of the revolution. However, as Villa was winning battles, it became clear that Villa and Carranza did not get along. Villa did not trust Carranza because he believed Carranza would become another dictator like Diaz and Huerta. As the dissension intensified between Villa and Carranza, Ángeles was perceived as anti-Carranza. A turning point occurred in May 1914, when General Panfilo Natera was ordered by Carranza to attack the City of Saltillo. When General Natera failed to take Saltillo, Carranza ordered Villa to loan General Natera 5,000 Villista soldiers, but Villa did want to loan Natera a sizable army. Natera had been a general under his command, and Villa knew that Natera did not have the ability to gain a victory at Saltillo. When Carranza insisted that Villa loan Natera soldiers, Villa sent Carranza a telegram stating he would rather resign than loan Natera 5,000 soldiers. At this point, Carranza believed the timing was right to get rid of Villa. He sent Villa a telegram accepting his resignation and instructed that the generals of the Division of the North get together to select whom among them would replace Villa. In response, it was Ángeles who sent Carranza a telegram with sharp language informing him that the generals had met and decided that Villa should continue to lead the Division of the North and if the selection of Villa was not accepted, then all the generals would resign. The action by Ángeles to support Villa only served to reinforce the view that Ángeles was anti-Carranza.

On his own initiative Villa went on to conquer Saltillo. His next battle was to take the City of Zacatecas, the last fortified city occupied by the forces of Huerta. Villa was delayed from attacking Zacatecas because Carranza withheld the coal he promised Villa to operate his military trains (coal deliveries came from the State of Coahuila, Carranza's home state). The action by Ángeles to support Villa only served to reinforce the view that Ángeles was anti-Carranza. The delaying tactics employed by Carranza made it possible for General Alvaro Obregon to arrive in Mexico City first, a tactical advantage for Carranza's claim to the Presidency of Mexico.

After Huerta was removed from the Presidency, the leaders of the Revolution met at the Convention of Aguascalientes, in the City of Aguascalientes, for the purpose of selecting a Provisional President. The key operatives at the Convention were, Ángeles, on behalf of Villa, and Obregon on behalf of Carranza. Unfortunately, the revolutionaries were not able to resolve their differences, and as a result, Villa and Carranza split into two permanent camps: Ángeles sided with Villa and Obregon sided with Carranza. From this point on it became a life and death struggle between Villa and Carranza to determine who would be the true leader of Mexico.

The turning point for Villa occurred in April 1915, when he lost two major battles against Obregon in the City of Celaya. When Villa was preparing for the attack on the City of Celaya, Ángeles, who was engaged in the State of Jalisco, cautioned Villa not to attack Celaya until he was able to bring up more artillery from Guadalajara. Villa ignored Ángeles's advice and proceeded to attack Celaya on March 9, and again on March 16, 1915. Villa was decisively defeated in the Battle for Celaya by General Alvaro Obregon. This was the second time that Villa had ignored the advice of Ángeles. In 1914, when Villa and Zapata had triumphantly entered Mexico City, Carranza retreated to oil rich Veracruz. Ángeles advised Villa to immediately attack Carranza at Veracruz because the Carranza troops were not organized, his back was against the sea, and Villa would reap the financial bonanza from the oil fields and customs house in the State of Veracruz. Villa rejected the advice of Ángeles because Villa felt he should protect the State of Jalisco, which was being threatened by the forces of Obregon.

Capture and Execution

After the defeat of Villa at Celaya, in 1915, Ángeles felt he needed time away from the Revolution and decided to move to the U.S. and settled in Texas, where he ran a dairy farm called El Bosque. After a few months in Texas, Angles sold the farm and moved to New York City, where he joined the Liberal Alliance Organization, a group of Mexican exiles. The Liberal Alliance believed that if the Revolution was not ended, the U.S. would occupy Mexico to protect American lives and business interests.

In 1918, Ángeles re-entered Mexico to meet with Villa to discuss the prospect of ending the Revolution. However, by this time Villa had experienced several military setbacks, had become an embittered person, and been reduced to fighting guerilla warfare. After several months in Chihuahua, Ángeles felt that Villa was not responsive to ending the Revolution and decided to return to his family. Ángeles departed on friendly terms with Villa, and Villa assigned him an escort of six men for his return to the U.S. On October 19, 1919, Ángeles was captured in the State of

110

Chihuahua, by Major Gabino Sandoval and a detachment of fifty Carranza soldiers. Ángeles was betrayed by Felix Salas, one of the escorts assigned by Villa. Salas was paid 6,000 pesos for leading Major Sandoval to where Ángeles was hidden. Ángeles was first sent to the City of Parral and then transferred to Chihuahua City for a military trial. As soon as Ángeles was captured, it was clear that Carranza intended to punish Ángeles, for several reasons: Carranza had not forgotten the embarrassment caused by Ángeles when the generals sent Carranza a telegram they would all resign if Villa was removed as the general to attack the City of Zacatecas, the decisive role of Ángeles at the Convention of Aguascalientes when Carranza was removed as the Primer Jefe, and the many causalities suffered by Carranza troops under artillery fire directed by Ángeles. The military charges against Ángeles were insubordination and rebellion against the Mexican Government and the Mexican Constitution. The military tribunal against Ángeles consisted of Carranza and Generals Gabriel Gavira, Gonzalo Escobar, Fernando Peraldi and Pablo Quiroga.

As soon as it was announced there would be a military trial, it was a forgone conclusion that Ángeles would be executed by order of Carranza. In reality, Carranza would have preferred that Major Sandoval had executed Ángeles when he was first captured, but now it was necessary to have a military trial as a showcase. After the capture of Ángeles, Carranza could not afford to have him summarily executed, such as was the case when he ordered the cold-blooded assassination of Zapata, only a few months earlier, at the Hacienda Chinemeca.

Since Carranza would have to find a more plausible way of removing Ángeles, he ordered that a court martial be convened in Chihuahua City. To ensure that public opinion did not gain any momentum against him, he ordered the proceedings be concluded in three days. The trial opened on November 26, 1919, at the

Teatro de los Heroes, the largest theatre in Chihuahua City. Many supporters, from both Mexico and the U.S., attended the trial. Lady auxiliary groups from the U.S. and Mexico offered financial assistance and moral support. Ángeles was found guilty and was executed before a firing squad on November 29. Ángeles died with dignity. At his trial, he declared he had returned to Mexico to find a way to end a revolution that had consumed too many lives and much loss of property. He defended Villa as being a "good man" who was led astray by the vulgarities of the Revolution. Over 5,000 attended his funeral procession.

The execution of Ángeles was a sham on the part of Carranza. Once again, Carranza proved that he was a dictator who was only interested in holding on to the Presidency by any means necessary. The sentiment of the nation was that Ángeles did not have to be executed, perhaps punished, but certainly not executed. Ángeles had been away from the Revolution for three years. When he returned to Mexico, he was not in uniform, not in charge of an army, had not made any declarations against the Carranza Government, and no Carranza soldiers had been killed due to the presence of Ángeles in the State of Chihuahua. Moreover, Ángeles had been a civilian for three years and was on his way to the United States. Many believed that Ángeles should have been prosecuted by a civil court, not a military court.

Ángeles was executed within three days of the verdict without an opportunity to seek an appeal. The execution of Ángeles and the assassination of Zapata have tainted Carranza's reputation as a dictator. Carranza could have sentenced Ángeles to prison for several years for insurrection, which would have allowed time for appeal and further judicial review. Execution within three days of the guilty verdict removed any opportunity for review of a final determination regarding the guilt of Ángeles.

Had Carranza done so, he would have gained a reputation as a statesman, rather than reinforce his standing as a dictator.

Chapter X.   Las Soldaderas of the Revolution

Las Soldaderas were women of the Mexican Revolution who served in the armies of Villa, Zapata, Obregón, Carranza, and to a lesser extent in the Federal Army[1]. Some historians have grossly underestimated the valuable contributions of the Soldaderas in military operations. Their role of supplying food and services to a marching army was critical because the armies of the Revolution did not have a formal military Quartermaster Service. The importance of having a supply line has been noted by many military historians, who have often stated that "an Army marches on its stomach." The absence of an adequate supply train had a devastating impact on Napoleon in 1804 and Adolph Hitler in 1942, when their armies invaded Russia during the cold of winter. Without an adequate supply of food, munitions, and winter clothing their soldiers starved and froze to death. This military blunder caused Napoleon and Hitler colossal defeats, in particular Hitler when General Von Paulus surrendered over 91,000 German soldiers at Stalingrad, of which only 5,000 ever returned to Germany.

Historians have generally referred to all women who fought in the Revolution as "Soldaderas"; however, there are some distinctions. The Soldaderas served in three capacities: as part of the Quartermaster Service providing food and services; as combatants on the front lines; or as in some cases, some women served both, in the Quartermaster Service and also performed combat duties. To facilitate describing their role in the Revolution,

---

[1] Federales or uniformed soldiers

115

we shall refer to women in the Quartermaster Service as Las Soldaderas del Campo (camp followers) and women that served in combat, as Soldaderas de Combate (women in combat).[2]

Soldaderas del Campo

The vast majority of women served the Revolution as Soldaderas del Campo. They travelled with the Revolutionary armies to forage food, cook meals, wash clothing and tended to the casualties of war. During combat, they provided nursing services to the wounded soldiers and also acted as ammo carriers[3]. Their participation allowed more soldiers to serve on the front lines, rather than being assigned to secure food and supplies needed by a marching army. In some cases they were the source of sexual companionship for their loved one who may have volunteered to join, or were forced to serve in the Revolution. The ability to attend to the wounded while in the field of battle served to save many lives. It also provided the soldiers with comfort knowing that a mother like care giver was tending to their needs when it mattered the most. Other Soldaderas took on the added responsibility of acting as spies because they could infiltrate an enemy camp to learn of the enemy's intentions, morale, troop strength, and armaments.

The respect and recognition the Soldaderas deserved did not come easy, as in the case of Beatriz Ortega, who managed to teach Pancho Villa a lesson in mercy. As a nurse, Beatriz was tending to

---

[2] Reséndez Fuentes, Andrés. "Battleground Women: Soldaderas and Female Soldiers in the Mexican Revolution." The Americas 51, 4 (April 1995).

[3] Soto, Shirlene Ann. Emergence of the Modern Mexican Woman. Denver, CO: Arden Press, 1990.

Federal and Villa troops who were wounded when Villa won the battle for the City of Zacatecas. Knowing that Villa executed the Federales, she removed their tell-tale military uniforms and refused to make a distinction between wounded Federales and Villistas, even after being threatened with death. Villa eventually treated Beatriz with respect. Her courage and humanity was etched in history when the State of Zacatecas dedicated a school bearing her name. [4]

More Soldaderas joined the ranks in the North with Villa and Carranza than in the South with Zapata. The North had larger armies and fought in the larger states of Chihuahua, Zacatecas, and Coahuila. In addition, their main method of transportation was by train, which offered faster deployment over larger geographic areas. In the South, Zapata fought with smaller armies and stayed mainly in the State of Morelos. Zapata's army tended to fight skirmishes near their ancestral villages so that his soldiers could return quickly to their homes to tend to their crops.

Many songs have been written about the bravery and exploits of the Soldaderas, such as "Adelita," "Juana Gallo," "Jesusita en Chihuahua," including the battle hymn "La Cucaracha" whenever Pancho Villa went into battle. The "La Adelita" is perhaps the most famous Soldadera song of the Revolution and was sung repeatedly when engaged in battle. It is the story of a young

---

[4] Macias, Anna. "Women and the Mexican Revolution, 1910-1920." The Americas 37, 1 (July 1980). Note: Although not related to the Revolution in time, Marisol Valles Garcia is a more recent example of a brave Mexican woman. In 2010, in the State of Guerrero she was affectionately called "La Adelita" because she was the only person brave enough to accept the position of Police Chief, after the previous Police Chief had been gunned down by a drug cartel.

woman in love with a sergeant and who travels with him throughout the Revolution. She not only cooked and cared for the wounded, but actually fought in battle. In time the word "Adelita" was generally applied to all the women who fought in the Revolution. It came to symbolize strength and courage. The song is supposed to be based on a real life character, whose identity has not been established. Some claim her real name was Altagracia Martinez, or perhaps Marieta Martinez. Others claim her real name was Adela Velarde, who actually took part in military action as a nurse.

The true source of La Adelita exploits cannot be easily determined, some of it is true action and some legendary. When the songs of the Revolution are taught to Mexican school age children, they learn Mexican history and the bravery of the Soldaderas. The real importance is that La Adelita legend is now part of Mexican culture and her fame is well known throughout Mexico. To wit, in contemporary Mexico, whenever there is cause for a celebration, a Mariachi Band is often requested to sing the songs of the Revolution. If a Mariachi Band is not able to sing the songs of the Revolution, it may find itself unemployed.

Soldaderas de Combate (combat)

The Soldaderas de Combate (combat) distinguished themselves for their bravery in battle because they served alongside the men in actual combat engagements. Some Soldaderas had such an outstanding combat record that they were allowed to form their own all female combat units. Margarita Neri was a Dutch-Mayan Indian woman from the State of Quintana Roo who became an officer under Zapata (Gomez). Margarita was a respected guerilla commander who led a force of 1,000, sweeping through the states of Tabasco and Chiapas looting, burning, and killing the Federal forces of Porfirio Diaz. Death and destruction are not unusual events during the time of war, except that this particular commander who was brandishing a machete and vowing to decapitate Diaz was a woman. Margarita earned such a reputation that the Governor of the State of Guerrero, upon hearing of her approach, hid in a crate and made a quick exit out of town.

Petra Herrera became a "Coronela" (Colonel) in Villa's army. She became famous for her bravery in the second battle in the taking the City of Torreon. She assumed the name of Pedro Herrera so she could fight along the men she commanded. She led a force of 200 men in blowing up bridges and was able to shut off the electricity, allowing Villa to enter the city undetected. After the battle for the City of Torreon, she let it be known that she was a female in disguise as a male soldier. Due to her leadership in Torreon, she was authorized to form her own unit of some 100 women soldiers. Later she served as a spy working as a bartender. Eventually she ran afoul of a bunch of drunken men who shot her and days later died from her wounds. Petra's involvement in the war effort was especially notable because of her strong leadership during combat operations in the field of battle. She successfully demonstrated that the power of women in combat could be just as effective as men[5].

Angela "Angel" Jimenez, who was born in Jalapa del Marquez in the State of Oaxaca, would become one of the bravest fighters against the Federales. When she was only fifteen years old, she witnessed an attempted rape of her sister by an officer searching for rebels in their home. Before the rape could take place, she grabbed the officer's gun and shot him. After this tragic event, Jimenez joined the Revolution to fight against the Federales. Disguised as a male soldier, she joined the army in hopes of finding peace and justice for her country. Jimenez served

---

[5] (Paniatowska-Salas) Poniatowska, Elena

in various roles, including soldier, flag bearer, explosives expert and spy. Though her appearance suggested she was a male soldier, Jimenez was not entirely disguised because the General of her troop knew her true identity as a female. Due to her gender, Jimenez had difficulty gaining recognition for her bravery; nonetheless, she was eventually promoted to Lieutenant. On one occasion, Jimenez was able to use her gender to her advantage. Upon being incarcerated, she was able to escape prison by dressing up in woman's clothing, and after she escaped prison, she formulated a plan for freeing her fellow prisoners. Jimenez also served as a spokesperson for the Soldaderas, defending their role in the Revolution. When General Amaro ordered that all women brigades be disbanded, she candidly stated, "I do not need to have the physical body of a male to be a brave soldier." Jimenez remained in the army for several years and later immigrated to the U.S.

Ramona Flores, also known as the "Tigress," commanded a group of 100 men. When General Felipe Ángeles, one of most outstanding generals of the Revolution, was passing through the City of Culiacan, she took the occasion to receive General Ángeles with an Honor Guard. She brought her men to attention, marched them around the parade grounds twice to demonstrate to General Ángeles that her men were disciplined and combat ready.

Elisa Griessen Zambrano was a school teacher who lived near the City of Parral, a Pancho Villa's stronghold. When cavalry troops under American Major Frank Tompkins arrived in Parral (part of the General Pershing's Punitive Expedition) to capture Pancho Villa, she became indignant that American troops had penetrated some 500 miles as far as Parral to capture Villa. She incited a riot against Carranza troops because they had allowed American troops deep in Mexico. She started the riot by throwing stones and voicing insults against Carranza troops, and would repeatedly shout "Viva Villa, Viva Mexico." When the situation got out of hand, the American troops retreated and started shooting at Carranza troops. The incident resulted in three Americans and ten Carranza soldiers killed. Her leadership forced the American troops to withdraw from Parral. The incident also created a furor in the U.S. because Pershing's troops were supposed to be fighting the Villistas, not the Mexican Army.

Although the Soldaderas served in great numbers in the Revolution, there was one exception. General Pancho Villa did not allow the Soldaderas to accompany the men of his elite cavalry, Los Dorados de Villa, into battle. Los Dorados was cavalry force of 200 men, handpicked by Villa for their bravery, horsemanship, and ability to shoot a rifle while attacking on horseback. They were noted for their daring cavalry charges during the heat of battle. One possible reason may have been that Villa did not want the Dorados to have any distractions before the going into battle. Another reason may have been that some soldiers became so enamored with their favorite Soldadera, that sometimes they would desert their post to be with their loved one.

Summary

The Mexican Revolution cannot be fully understood without discussing the role of the Soldaderas. They served along the front lines next to the fighting men, they shared the same time and space. They endured the hardships of being in battle, not knowing if they would survive to live another day. They provided comfort and companionship, and in some cases experienced child birth under dire conditions. One must remember the Soldaderas were wives, mothers, or daughters who fought in the Revolution because they believed in a better Mexico. Without a doubt, they had to be very brave to volunteer for a struggle that promised nothing except the opportunity to break the back of tyrants and rid Mexico of economic slavery and peonage.

There is no record of how many Soldaderas died or were injured in combat. Considering the Revolution lasted ten years and they constantly served on the front lines, we can be sure that many of them died, were injured, or were killed in battle. Ironically, while many larger than life monuments have been constructed to honor generals such as Villa, Zapata, Obregón, we know of only a few modest renderings honoring the Soldaderas of the Revolution. The oft repeated photo images of anonymous women marching alongside their soldiers, whether on foot or horseback, or sitting on top of railroad cars on the way to battle, is insufficient recognition for the Soldaderas of the Revolution.

Las Soldaderas of the Revolution

They served as the Quartermaster Corps in the armies of the Revolution. They foraged for food, carried ammunition, loaded rifles, attended to the wounded, and provided comfort to their loved ones. Some Soldaderas even served as front line soldiers.

Chapter XI.   The Convention of Aguascalientes

In July 1914, Victoriano Huerta left for Europe after being defeated by the forces of Carranza, Obregón, Villa, and Zapata. It was now time for the Revolutionary leaders to debate the future of Mexico. According to an arrangement arrived a several months earlier, the generals agreed to hold a convention in the City of Aguascalientes. Accordingly, on October 14, 1914, one hundred fifty military leaders gathered at Aguascalientes to decide who should be the leader of Mexico, until formal elections could be held to elect a new Mexican President.

The ground rules for the convention were that only military leaders could attend, and only one representative for each 1,000 soldiers would be allowed. The City of Aguascalientes was selected because it was neutral territory, a small state, and not represented by a major military leader. To facilitate discussion, neither Carranza nor Villa was allowed to participate in the day-to-day deliberations. This, however, did not preclude Carranza or Villa to engage in behind the scenes posturing and advocacy. Villa, in a display of bravado, informed the Convention that he and Carranza should resign and have a pistol duel to determine who would survive the Revolution. Carranza, the more pragmatic of the two, informed the Convention that he and Villa should resign, and he would leave the country for ten days. It is doubtful that either of the two was willing to give up their power base and lose control of their respective army. Generals Alvaro Obregón and Felipe Ángeles played a crucial role in keeping the Convention focused on the main issues. Obregón was the lead spokesperson for Carranza, and Ángeles was spokesperson for Villa. At first, Zapata did not want to participate in the

Convention, however Ángeles rendered a valuable service to the Convention when he made a special trip to the State of Morelos and was able to convince Zapata that it was his obligation for his representatives to be involved in discussing the issues of the Revolution.

After several days of debate and controversy, the generals voted to remove Carranza as the Primer Jefe. They elected Eulalio Gutierrez as the Provisional President and requested Obregón, a supporter of Carranza, to contact Carranza in Veracruz and advise him he had been voted out as Primer Jefe. Carranza refused to receive Obregón and also refused to resign as the Primer Jefe, on the basis that the convention was not a legally constituted body, and therefore, the Convention did not have the authority to remove him as the Primer Jefe. On November 10, 1914, Provisional President Gutierrez informed Carranza he had ten days to accept the recommendation of the Convention, but again Carranza refused to resign. His negative response caused the Convention to split into two permanent camps. The Carranza and Obregón faction became the Constitutionalists, who believed they were acting in accordance with the Constitution of Mexico. Gutiérrez, Villa, and Zapata became the Conventionists, who believed that the Aguascalientes Convention was the true instrument of peace and the will of the people. Villa was named as the commander of all Revolutionary forces by Provisional President Gutierrez, which of course infuriated Carranza. From this point on, Carranza and Villa became bitter enemies and engaged in some of the bloodiest battles of the Revolution to determine who would be the leader of Mexico.

Conflicts between Villa and Carranza

It is difficult to establish with clarity and certainty why the Revolutionary leaders could not resolve their differences. Several historians have offered different interpretations. Perhaps a summary of the interaction between Villa and Carranza will be useful in understanding the events at Aguascalientes:

- Carranza coveted the Presidency and he was not about to yield the power he had claimed when he declared himself as the Primer Jefe under the Plan de Guadalupe in 1913. Carranza's main goal was to stay in power and therefore he insisted that Villa and Zapata acknowledge they were subordinate to his authority.

- Villa was not inclined to yield the power he wielded as the General of the Division del Norte. Villa wanted Carranza to recognize that his Division was an independent army that would operate in concert with Carranza, but not subordinate to him. Villa asserted that he was personally responsible for developing and organizing the Division when he fought against the forces of Porfirio Diaz in 1910, Pascual Orozco in 1911, and Victoriano Huerta in 1913. Villa believed his ability to organize, supply, and pay for his army entitled him to be treated as an independent army. Moreover, Villa made it clear to Carranza that his militia was the largest force in the Revolution, and his army was winning the greatest battles of the Revolution.

- During the campaign to defeat Huerta, a genuine dislike developed between Villa and Carranza. Carranza believed that Villa was undermining his status as the leader of Mexico because he was gaining fame by winning all the major battles of the Revolution, and this interfered with Carranza's plan to become President of Mexico. Carranza initiated a program of defamation against Villa. He let it be known that Villa was not qualified to be a general, he was insubordinate, failed to follow orders, and used excessive force when confiscating crops, livestock, and land from the Hacendados and foreign investors. On the other hand, Villa chose not to subjugate himself to Carranza because he believed Carranza was becoming another dictator, much like Diaz and Huerta.

- Villa maintained he needed to continue confiscating property from the Hacendados to pay his soldiers, supplies, arms, and munitions. Carranza, a wealthy landowner, wanted Villa to limit his aggressiveness in confiscating property. Although Carranza objected to Villa's program of confiscating property, he did not offer an alternative on how Villa was to supply and pay for his army.

- As Carranza and Villa marched south to Mexico City to remove Huerta, and claim the leadership of Mexico, it was clear that Villa's army would arrive in Mexico City first. To prevent Villa from arriving at Mexico City, Carranza ordered Villa to loan General Panfilo Natera soldiers to attack the City of Saltillo. Villa refused because Saltillo would take him 150 miles away from his line of march. Villa informed Carranza that Saltillo was in the war zone of General Pablo Gonzalez, and thus,

General Gonzalez should be ordered to attack Saltillo.

- Villa was quite aware of Carranza's tactic to delay his rapid movement to Mexico City; nonetheless, Villa was willing to work with Carranza as the Primer Jefe. On his own initiative, in July 1915, Villa attacked and defeated the Federal troops in Saltillo. Villa now planned an attack on the City of Zacatecas, but Carranza would have none of this. To ensure that Villa did not get to Mexico City first, he denied Villa the coal he had promised for Villa to attack Zacatecas.

The Convention was the last opportunity to bring peace to the nation. Villa and Carranza became engaged in a struggle to the end, or until one camp or the other was totally defeated. During the next two years the nation witnessed some of the bloodiest battles of the Revolution. In retrospect, it was a national tragedy that neither Carranza nor Villa could put aside their differences to bring about peace. Their egos were more important than the stated purpose of the Convention to resolve the issues of the Revolution. Perhaps Carranza could have taken the initiative to step aside. After all, when he installed himself as the Primer Jefe, it was to ensure the defeat of Huerta. He could have acknowledged that he was not elected to the Presidency by an electoral process, and, since Huerta had now been defeated, it was reasonable to expect that he was no longer critical for him to serve as the Primer Jefe. Carranza should have taken into consideration that he named himself as Primer Jefe as a temporary measure. The Plan de Guadalupe, which he initiated in his home State of Coahuila, was accepted by the Revolutionaries for the sole purpose of removing Huerta. Moreover, the plan that Carranza formulated was essentially a local document that was signed by a military dignitary of no higher rank than Colonel. Carranza should have been perceptive enough to understand that the nation needed a neutral person to lead the nation provisionally until formal elections could be held.

Carranza, an aristocrat could not fathom that Villa had no ambition of becoming the President of Mexico. Villa had stated several times to his intimates that he could never be President because he did not have the education and diplomatic finesse to lead the nation. Instead, he had often mentioned that General Felipe Ángeles should be elected as President. Ángeles was an outstanding artillery officer, well educated, and accepted as a person of integrity and credibility.

In the final analysis, the Convention failed in its mission because Carranza refused to abide by the decision of the Revolutionaries that he resign as Primer Jefe. Carranza was being hypocritical when he told the Convention that they did not have the authority to remove him. He had been a willing participant in the planning of the Convention months earlier, and was well represented by his loyal general Alvaro Obregón. However, when the vote went against him, he found it expedient to reject the outcome of the Convention on the pretense that they did not have the authority to remove him as Primer Jefe. It was clear that it was more important for him to remain as the Primer Jefe and exercise the power he coveted, without the benefit of a free electoral process.

Carranza clearly understood he had the fate of the Revolution in the palm of his hands. He failed to put aside his ambition for power. Few men at such a critical point in history have been asked to make such a sacrifice in the best interest of the nation. In this endeavor, he failed. Unfortunately for Mexico, Carranza fell in step like so many of other dictators before him who had occupied the Presidency by sheer force and once established as a dictator, they could not be removed by peaceful means.

Carranza's tenure as Primer Jefe involved the bloodiest battles of the Revolution. By trying to subjugate Villa, he made the mistake of trying to tame a tiger that was used to survival by cunning and instinct. Carranza could not accept the fact that Villa was a unique and independent general. Carranza believed that Villa was below his standard of civility and was not qualified to be a "General" under his command.

Chapter XII.   Attack on Columbus, New Mexico

On March 9, 1916, at three in the morning, Pancho Villa and some 350 Villistas attacked Columbus, New Mexico, a small village three miles from the Mexican border.

There are three theories why Villa attacked Columbus. The most widely accepted theory is that Villa attacked Columbus in retaliation against the U.S. for having sided with the forces of Venustiano Carranza. Another theory is that Villa attacked Columbus because he wanted to get even with the merchant Sam Ravel, who supposedly got paid by Villa to provide supplies that were not delivered. Yet another theory alleges that German agents paid Villa, so war could be started between Mexico and the U.S., thus delaying U.S. entry in World War I. Empirical evidence does not support the last two theories. Prior to the attack on Columbus, there was no mention by Villa, or his compatriots, of Sam Ravel regarding supplies that were not delivered. Similarly, there was no mention of German agents meeting with Villa to offer him money to attack Columbus.

It is clear that Villa was irritated with President Wilson for siding more than once with Carranza. After Villa was decisively defeated in the two battles for Celaya in April 1915, President Wilson made a diplomatic decision to recognize Carranza as the de facto President of Mexico. The action by President Wilson to recognize Carranza changed the balance of power between Carranza and Villa. When Carranza declared himself Primer Jefe in 1913, he had not been elected President by a democratic process and therefore the country was still divided regarding the true leadership of the nation. Moreover, when President Wilson granted Carranza recognition, Villa and Carranza were engaged in some of the greatest battles of the Revolution, the outcome of which would determine who would lead the nation.

The de facto recognition by President Wilson reinforced Carranza's standing with foreign governments and other revolutionary forces. President Wilson also authorized the sale of arms and munitions for Carranza but placed an embargo on Villa. This made it more difficult for Villa to purchase munitions from American arms dealers, and, if he could obtain them, he would have to pay a higher price. The most grievous action taken by President Wilson, which could be construed as an act of war, was to authorize the use of eight military trains by the U.S. Army to transport 5,000 Carranza troops to Douglas, Arizona on American soil. The military trains travelled over 1,000 miles from Laredo and Eagle Pass, Texas to Douglas to arrive in time to defeat Villa at Agua Prieta, Sonora. When the Carranza troops arrived at Douglas, they simply walked across the street to Agua Prieta. Thus, when Villa planned his attack on Agua Prieta he expected to face 1,500 Carranza troops. Instead he faced 6,500 Carranza troops, courtesy of the U.S. Army.

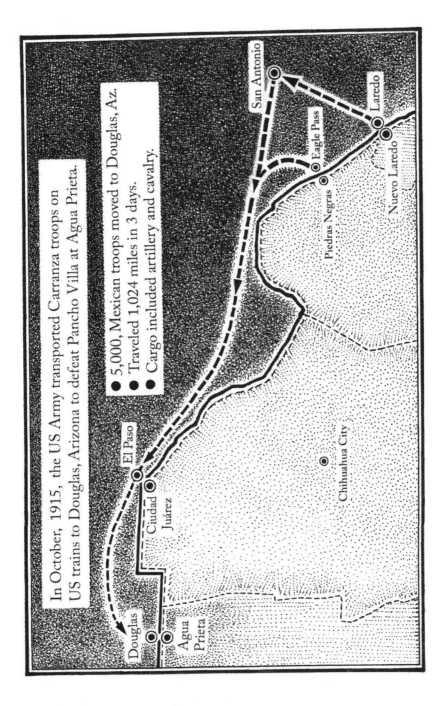

In October, 1915, the US Army transported Carranza troops on US trains to Douglas, Arizona to defeat Pancho Villa at Agua Prieta.

- 5,000, Mexican troops moved to Douglas, Az.
- Traveled 1,024 miles in 3 days.
- Cargo included artillery and cavalry.

San Antonio

Laredo

Eagle Pass

Piedras Negras

Nuevo Laredo

El Paso

Ciudad Juárez

Chihuahua City

Douglas

Agua Prieta

During the first years of the Revolution, from 1910 to 1912, Villa was allowed to buy all the arms and munitions he needed to prosecute the Revolution against Pascual Orozco and Victoriano Huerta. Also, whenever the U.S. Government asked that American lives and property be protected, Villa always provided a positive response. In addition, several American Generals met with Villa at the border to take pictures with him and complement him on his victories and military tactics. Now that the U.S. had sided with Carranza, Villa was bitter and felt he had been betrayed. He found himself in the position of having to fight on two fronts, the forces of Carranza, and the influence of the U.S. Government.

Although Villa had retribution in mind, it is not clear why Villa selected the village of Columbus to vent his dissatisfaction with President Wilson. Columbus was a small hamlet with 1,300 inhabitants, as well as the troopers of the Tenth Cavalry Regiment. The Tenth Cavalry was known as the Buffalo Soldiers because it was made up of segregated black soldiers who wore black jackets made of buffalo skin. The hamlet had only one bank and three hotels and two general stores, and was not considered a major military outpost. The historical evidence suggests that Villa attacked Columbus to seek vengeance against President Wilson. Moreover, he was at the end of his tether and needed to make a personal statement against Carranza and President Wilson.

The Revolution was losing its luster, and Villa was losing ground and prestige. He had to change the existing paradigm to reduce the influence of Carranza and Wilson over the conduct of the Revolution. He needed to introduce a new set of dynamics to keep his followers from deserting his ranks and at the same time allow him to recruit Villistas (followers of Villa). Columbus was convenient because it was only three miles from the Mexican border and offered a quick escape route. Villa was aware that an attack on Columbus would violate the honor and prestige of the U.S. It would also create a major problem for Carranza because the U.S. would conclude that Carranza was unable to contain Villa, and it would hold Carranza accountable for being unable to secure the border. The combined reaction would provide Villa the notoriety he needed and thus revive his fortunes of war.

It does not appear the attack was adequately planned. Some Villistas infiltrated the hamlet the day before, but apparently the intelligence they brought back was faulty. They did not correctly assess the strength of the Tenth Cavalry. If the Villistas had spent more time evaluating their primary and secondary targets, they would have correctly identified the deployment of the Cavalry troops.

The Attack

In preparation for the attack and their escape, the Villistas cut a large segment of the border fence. On the morning on March 9, 1916, about 350 Villistas formed in three columns to attack from three different directions and eventually converge at the center of the hamlet. One column with 90 men was commanded by Colonel Francisco Beltran; a second with 80 men by Colonel Fernandez and a third with 90 by Colonel Pablo Lopez. A fourth column with 90 men would remain nearby in reserve. The Villistas started the attack at dawn, Villa's favorite mode of attack, and while his soldiers played "La Cucaracha." Within minutes they were receiving return machine gun fire from the U.S. cavalry. After two hours of battle, the Villistas were forced to retreat when they recognized they were up against superior gunfire. In the ensuing gun battle, the Villistas killed 10 civilians and 8 troopers. During the skirmish, 30 Villistas were killed and 17 were captured. The

Tenth Cavalry pursued Villa's troops for several miles into Chihuahua. During the escape, another 25 Villistas were killed or wounded. (See map of Villa's evasion route at end of chapter.)

After the attack, Villa knew he had to move quickly into the mountains of Chihuahua where the terrain favored guerrilla warfare. On the first day, the Villistas reached Arroyo Gato, 16 miles from Columbus. The second day they were at Ascencion, 70 miles away. On the third day, they arrived at the Hacienda Corralitos, 100 miles from Columbus. At Corralitos, a large Hacienda owned by E. D. Morgan, they confiscated fresh horses and food supplies. They left for Galeana, 140 miles further, then on to El Valle, 170 miles away. At each stop, Villa was pressed to obtain more conscripts, horses, and food supplies. Within a week he arrived at the large town of Namiquipa, 240 miles south. Here Villa had many compatriots, and the village was the home of his loyal general, Candelario Cervantes.

At Namiquipa they were strong enough to defeat a garrison of Carranza troops where they captured 40 prisoners, 100 horses, 2 machine guns, and 100 rifles. As Villa retreated further south from Namiquipa, he was almost half way to Parral, Chihuahua, and his favorite hiding place. He was gaining confidence and acquiring the munitions and supplies he would surely need when the American Army would come in hot pursuit. Villa's escape into the mountains of Chihuahua was a situation he had experienced twenty years before when he shot the Hacendado Luis Negrete and had to team up with Parra and Alvarado to live as fugitives in the mountains of Chihuahua and Durango.

Conspiracy to Annihilate Pancho Villa

Most historians have concluded that the *main reason* for organizing the Punitive Expedition was to punish Pancho Villa for attacking Columbus, New Mexico. Based on recent research conducted by the authors of *Viva Villa*, we do not concur with this conclusion. The authors would argue the Punitive Expedition was organized as a conspiracy by President Wilson, the U.S. Army, and Carranza to cover up the use of military trains by the U.S. Army to defeat Pancho Villa in the Battle for Agua Prieta. The use of military trains to transport 5,000 Carranza troops was an act of war on the part of the U.S. Government that involved certain risk, as evidenced by the reaction by Pancho Villa against President Wilson when he attacked Columbus.

Since Pancho Villa was not eliminated at Agua Prieta, the U.S. Army had to be concerned that eventually the American public would learn that President Wilson and the U.S. Army had conspired to defeat Pancho Villa at Agua Prieta, and they could not afford for the American public to learn about an international covert operation. Most Americans believe that a struggle for leadership should be played on a level playing field, and would not support covert operations to interfere in a legitimate revolution of a neighboring country.

When Villa attacked Columbus, President Wilson and the U.S. Army saw a second opportunity (after Agua Prieta) to liquidate Villa. They were aware that the American public has a short memory. If they were successful in quickly annihilating Villa, the American public would soon forget the covert operation at Agua Prieta. They would focus on the fact that Villa had been eliminated, and he was made to pay for the Columbus raid.

The author's reasoning that a conspiracy existed is based on (1) military intelligence by General Hugh Scott, (2) U.S. military

139

de-capitation doctrine to remove an obstacle to U.S. national interest, (3) the size of the military force, (4) the rapidity in mobilizing the expedition, and (5) the arbitrary entry by the U.S. Army into Mexico.

(1) **Military Intelligence.** On January 5, 1915, General Hugh Scott, Commanding General, U.S. Army called for a meeting along the border between the U.S. Army, Pancho Villa, and Jose Maytorena, the Governor of the State of Sonora. The troops of Governor Maytorena were engaged against the troops of Carranza along the U.S.–Mexico border in Sonora and General Scott was concerned that stray bullets would cause death to U.S. Army troops and citizens along the border. At this juncture in the Revolution, Pancho Villa was at the apex of his military career and General Scott wanted him to help mediate the potential damage at the border. From the meeting, it was agreed that Governor Maytorena's troops would move away from the border, and the Carranza troops would redeploy to Agua Prieta. Thus, as early as January 1915, General Scott was fully aware that the strength of Carranza troops was concentrated at Agua Prieta.

(2) **Decapitation.** In 2004, Victor D. Hyder, Lieutenant Commander, United States Navy conducted a study regarding U.S. Army military doctrine regarding decapitation[6]. Lt. Commander Hyder noted that decapitation is employed when the U.S. Government decides to eliminate a target that is not in the best interest of U.S. national power. According to Hyder,

---

[6] "Decapitation Operations: Criteria for Targeting Enemy Leadership", 2004

"The United States assisted the defenders of Agua Prieta with trainloads of U.S. and Mexican reinforcements, artillery, munitions, and equipment. Americans helped convert Agua Prieta from a small port city into an impregnable fortress prior to Villa's attack." It is reasonable to assume that the plan to use military trains came from General Scott because he knew from the January 1915 meeting with Villa, that the 1,500 Carranza troops at Agua Prieta were not sufficient to repel a determined attack by Villa. Thus, the planning, organizing, and transportation of the Mexican Army on U.S. soil and U.S. trains was most likely the brainchild of General Scott, specifically designed to defeat Villa at Agua Prieta.

(3) **The size of the military force.** Organizing a military force of over 10,000 troops clearly demonstrates the U.S. wanted to destroy Villa as soon as possible. The military orders given to General Pershing specifically stated he was to capture Pancho Villa or disband his army. Never in the history of the U.S. Army have orders been given to a field grade general to capture a targeted individual. Generals in the U.S. Army are usually given general orders that will allow them freedom of action consistent with meeting their military objective. In this case, the 10,000 man army was deployed for one single purpose – the destruction of Pancho Villa. In the final analysis, one can reasonably conclude that it does not take 10,000 soldiers to catch one so-called "bandit."

(4) **Rapidity in Mobilization.** Villa attacked Columbus on March 9, 1916, and by March 16, the U.S. Army had over 10,000 troops mobilized to enter Mexico.

Mobilization of such a large army involved a great deal of logistics to provision a large army. This included trucks, cavalry horses, feed for horses, and equipment, munitions, and food supplies for an extended military campaign. All of this was accomplished in a matter of a few days at prohibitive cost to the U.S. taxpayers. Again, this demonstrates the U.S. government was determined to eliminate Villa as soon as possible.

(5) **Arbitrary entry into Mexico.** Within one week of the attack on Columbus, the U.S. entered Mexico with a formidable force to capture Villa. The U.S. made no effort to coordinate the punitive expedition with the Carranza government. The U.S. simply entered Mexico, a sovereign nation, and told Carranza they were there to capture Villa, and essentially he had no say so in the matter. It is ironic that the U.S. would enter Mexico without Carranza's approval, considering that only four months earlier President Wilson had recognized Carranza as the de facto leader of the Government of Mexico, and had provided him with military trains to destroy Villa at Agua Prieta. When President Wilson granted Carranza de facto recognition, one would assume that the two national leaders had enjoyed a certain level of trust between each other, and international protocols would be respected between the two countries.

When Villa attacked Agua Prieta he faced 6,500 Carranza troops, not the 1.500 he expected. The intent of the U.S. Army was to ensure the complete collapse of Villa's Army at Agua Prieta. If the U.S. was sincere in capturing Villa it had several options: (1) organize a joint military operation with Carranza troops (after all, Carranza had ordered Gen. Obregon to capture Villa, dead or alive), (2) request extradition of Villa and assist Carranza in capturing Villa, or (3) the American generals, Hugh Scott, Fredrick Funston and John Pershing, could have called on Villa for a meet and confer resolution. These generals knew Villa well and conferred with him several times to settle border disputes involving skirmishes at the border.

The attack on Columbus took President Wilson by complete surprise, but his reaction was quick and forceful. On March 10, 1916, just one day following the attack, Secretary of War Newton Baker issued the following military order to capture Pancho Villa:

> "You will promptly organize an adequate military force of troops under the command of Brigadier General Pershing and will direct him to proceed promptly across the border in Pursuit of the *Mexican band* which attacked the town of Columbus ... These troops will be withdrawn to American territory as soon as the de facto government of Mexico is able to relieve them of this work. In any event the work of these troops will be regarded as finished as soon as *Villa band*, or bands are known to be broken up ..."

[Italics added by authors]

The logistics for organizing the expedition were assigned to General Fredrick Funston, who was in charge of American troops along the Mexican border. The expedition was placed under the command of General John Pershing, who was known as Black Jack Pershing because two of his regiments were made up of segregated black troopers. In the U.S. Army, Cavalry personnel are referred to as "troopers" because they use horses for transportation, compared to a Ground Infantry Regiment, where they are referred to as "foot soldiers." Pershing was a West Point graduate who had served with distinction fighting in the Indian

Wars, Cuba in 1898, and against the Moro Insurrectionists in the Philippines in 1905. The Pershing expedition was a formidable army of over 10,000 soldiers that included the following order of battle:

- Seventh Cavalry
- Tenth Cavalry
- Eleventh Cavalry
- Sixteenth Infantry
- Seventeenth Infantry
- Two Batteries from the Sixth Field Artillery

The First Aero Squadron, Commanded by Captain Benjamin Foulois, was also attached to provide air reconnaissance on Villa's movements and to maintain communications between Pershing and his superiors at Fort Bliss, Texas. The Aero Squadron consisted of eight Curtiss JN-3 airplanes, commonly referred to "Jennies." This was the first time an air force had been used in warfare. The Jennies were not very successful in conducting reconnaissance missions. The pilots were inexperienced and their engines were underpowered and unable to navigate the air streams in the mountains of Chihuahua. Their main function was to conduct air surveillance and fly communiqués from Pershing's field operations to headquarters staff at Fort Bliss, Texas.

The expedition also included a young Lieutenant by the name of George Smith Patton, who later was to become one of America's top generals in World War W II. Actually, Lt. Patton was not scheduled to join the expedition, but he wanted to go so badly that he made a special appeal to General Pershing. The General, while stationed at Fort Bliss, met the Patton family and fell in love with Nitta Patton, Patton's sister. The year before the

General had lost his wife and three of his children in a fire at the Presidio Army Camp in San Francisco. His four year old son, Warren, was the only survivor. Lt. Patton was to be a temporary aide, but he and the General got along so well, that Patton served as a confidant for the remainder of the expedition.

Pershing crossed into Mexico in March 1916, with over 10,000 troops. He was instructed not to occupy any of the villages or towns and not to use the railroad system of Mexico to transport troops. His supply train was overwhelming, consisting of horses, supply wagons, Dodge Trucks, and a Medical Unit large enough to support a large invasion force.

Pershing initiated an aggressive campaign to capture Villa, but Villa was always one step ahead. He employed several Americans as scouts who had lived in Mexico for several years who spoke fluent Spanish. Because Pershing had little success in tracking Villa, he received approval to add Apache Scouts from Arizona who were regarded as excellent trackers. President Wilson and Secretary Baker believed that the Mexican people were going to welcome the American troops with arms wide open; however, this was not to be the case. The Americans quickly learned that in Villa, they were up against an experienced and determined guerrilla fighter. Most of the time, the villagers treated Pershing's troops with hostility and refused to sell Pershing food and supplies. The villages supported Villa by creating diversionary tactics, such as giving false information, misdirection as to the whereabouts of Villa, set up false trails and by cutting telephone lines.

The expedition was further hampered by the hostility on the part of Primer Jefe Venustiano Carranza, who made it clear that he did not approve the presence of American troops on Mexican soil. He instructed his commanders not to allow Pershing troops to advance any further south than Parral, Chihuahua. Although Pershing commanded a superior military force, he was never able to catch sight of nor capture Villa. He came close on one or two occasions when Pershing troops engaged the Villistas in their hideouts. However, whenever Pershing got close, Villa's scouts made sure Villa was one step ahead. There were only two skirmishes where gunfire was exchanged between American and Mexican soldiers, at Parral and Carrizal. However, these skirmishes were between the troops of Pershing and the troops of Carranza. Perhaps, the firefights that occurred between Pershing and Carranza is what Villa had in mind when he attacked Columbus, New Mexico. Pershing exceeded his military orders when he engaged Carranza troops. His orders were explicit regarding the capture of Pancho Villa.

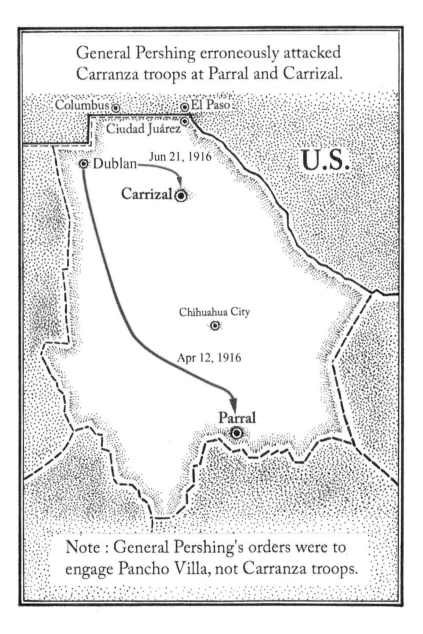

General Pershing erroneously attacked Carranza troops at Parral and Carrizal.

Columbus · El Paso · Ciudad Juárez · Dublan · Jun 21, 1916 · Carrizal · U.S. · Chihuahua City · Apr 12, 1916 · Parral

Note : General Pershing's orders were to engage Pancho Villa, not Carranza troops.

Confrontation at Parral

On April 12, 1916, U.S. Army Major Frank Tompkins arrived at
Parral presumably to purchase food and forage but actually
looking for the elusive Villa. Major Tompkins commanded 100
troopers and was known to harbor hostility towards Mexicans.
His antagonism ran even deeper considering that the Seventh
Calvary, the defenders of Columbus, was taken by Villa's surprise
attack. Moreover, by this time, U.S. troops had penetrated 500
miles into the interior of Mexico with no tangible results.
Tompkins believed he needed to capture Villa to redeem himself
and restore his reputation with the U.S. army. Tompkins was
escorted to the headquarters of General Ismael Lozano and the
Mayor of Parral. Tompkins was advised by General Lozano that
his troops were not welcomed and he should leave. Tompkins
said he would leave as soon as he received food and forage for his
horses. By this time a pro Villista crowd, led by Elisa Griessen
Zambrano, was throwing stones and shouting "Villa Viva" and
"Viva Mexico." As the troops retreated, someone in the crowd
fired at the troopers. Tompkins returned to contact General
Lozano about the crowd's hostility. General Lozano responded by
having his soldiers disperse the crowd of instigators, who
immediately turned their anger on Lozano's soldiers. In the melee,
General Lozano urged Tompkins to leave Parral, but Tompkins
again refused. Instead Tompkins ordered his troopers to fire at the
Carranza soldiers. Tompkins initiated a slow retreat to the small
village of Santa Cruz de Villegas, two miles from Parral.

At Santa Cruz, General Lozano made a second attempt to
have Tompkins leave Parral under a flag of truce, or his soldiers
would attack in full force. Again Tompkins refused to leave
Parral. However, a major battle was averted when Colonel Brown

arrived with a detachment of the Tenth Cavalry to rescue Tompkins. In the engagement, three American troopers and 8 Carranza troops were killed, and a number of wounded.

Pershing, who had set up camp at Satevo, near Parral, Chihuahua, learned of the skirmish as soon as it happened when several of the cavalry troopers who had escaped reported to his encampment. After the incident, Pershing ordered another 700 troops and supplies to reinforce Parral in the event of further armed conflict with Carranza troops. Unable to catch Villa, and now facing armed resistance from Carranza, Pershing requested military approval to occupy all of the State of Chihuahua. His request was denied. Other military minds of the expedition proposed a second invasion to depart from Texas to occupy all of Mexico, but this request was also denied.

President Wilson now realized that a military intrusion over 500 miles into Mexico, reaching as far as the State of Durango, was fraught with risk. If another skirmish like Parral were to occur, involving the death of soldiers and civilians, Carranza would be forced to declare war against the U.S. In addition, President Wilson was hard pressed to explain to the American public why he needed 10,000 troops to capture one individual by the name of Pancho Villa.

In an effort to resolve the escalating conflict, President Wilson arranged for a meeting at the international border at El Paso, Texas, between Generals Fredrick Funston and Hugh Scott and Mexican General Alvaro Obregón. During this period, American egos, craving for "good" news about the success of the expedition, were being satisfied by a number of newspaper and magazine journalists who travelled with the expedition. On the other hand, several newspapers in El Paso that were sympathetic towards the Revolution and Villa were being suppressed. The government did not want Mexicans and Mexican-Americans to become incited over the negativism regarding American troops in Mexico.

The Generals met at El Paso and agreed on the following points: after Villa had been destroyed or disbursed, Carranza was to gain control of the border; U.S. troops would withdraw from Mexico; and Carranza was not to impede the movement of Pershing's troops. When the agreement was forwarded to Carranza for approval, he found the agreement unacceptable. He demanded that the U.S. troops withdraw immediately, or there would be military confrontations. Carranza insisted that if his demands were not met, he would blockade any further military movements into the interior of Mexico. In view of Carranza's strong position, the U.S. opted to partially withdraw Pershing's troops. Pershing was instructed to return to the initial starting line at Colonia Dublan, a Mormon settlement near Columbus, New Mexico. In addition Pershing was instructed to avoid any more skirmishes. He was advised not to be concerned with any issues regarding the honor and prestige of the U.S.

Confrontation at Carrizal

By June, tension between the two countries continued to escalate. General Jacinto Trevino, commander of Carranza forces in Chihuahua, sent Pershing a clear-cut message not to deploy troops any further south of Parral, Chihuahua, and, if troops were encountered, they would be fired upon. To ensure that Pershing understood the seriousness of the directive, General Jacinto Trevino sent officers to visit Pershing to review the meaning and intent of his message. Pershing replied he was not under any orders to restrict his pursuit of the *bandits* [italics added]. Pershing further indicated that if his forces were fired upon, Trevino would be responsible for any resulting military action. Matters were now deteriorating rapidly between the two governments. President Wilson ordered four more states to activate their militia, and he ordered sixteen warships to the coast of Mexico.

After the skirmish at Parral, Pershing was under strict orders to hold his troops in the vicinity of Colonia Dublan. Nonetheless, Pershing ordered two cavalry patrols to the village of Villa Ahumada, about eighty miles to the east. Villa Ahumada is located on the main highway leading to Chihuahua City, the capitol of the state. The patrols were sent to Villa Ahumada because Pershing received intelligence reports that Carranza had some 10,000 troops in the area. Captain Charles Boyd was in charge of Troop C and Captain Lewis Morey was in charge of Troop K. Both were West Point graduates. The patrols arrived near Carrizal on June 21 a few miles from Villa Ahumada. Captain Boyd was cautioned by his own officers to be careful when entering Carrizal since there was no need for another skirmish like the one at Parral. Boyd then decided to prepare a written request for approval to travel through Carrizal; however, before the note could be delivered, he was met by the local commander who told Boyd he could not proceed any farther.

As a ruse, Boyd told the commander that he was pursuing an army deserter and some bandits. As this discussion was taking place, General Felix Gomez arrived to discuss Boyd's military orders. Boyd gave the same story regarding an army deserter and bandits. General Gomez did not believe Boyd and told him that if he proceeded any further, he would be fired upon. Boyd answered that he was obligated to comply with his military orders to march through Carrizal. As Boyd moved his troops forward, he immediately began to receive fire from the Carranza troops. The skirmish lasted most of the day; 12 U.S. troopers were killed, 12 wounded and 24 were taken prisoners. The prisoners were taken to Villa Ahumada and later transferred to the City of Juarez at the border. Within days after their capture, Carranza allowed the American prisoners to be returned to the U.S. After the Carrizal incident, President Wilson asked Congress for additional troops to be assigned to the border. He declared that Mexico had no formal government, because Carranza had not been elected, but rather he had imposed himself as the Primer Jefe. President Wilson stated that if Mexico did have a formal government, he would have asked Congress for a declaration of war. The skirmish at Parral could have evolved into a major battle, with many more Americans killed if the Carranza troops had stayed on the offensive. They had superior numbers and were in control of the terrain. However, it is clear that Carranza did not want to engage in an all-out war that he was sure he could not win.

The Carrizal incident was a severe setback for President Wilson, especially when his own army investigators informed him that Captain Boyd was responsible for instigating the skirmish. General Pershing was also hard pressed to explain why he had sent patrols so far west near Chihuahua City; contrary to the orders he had received to keep his troops near Colonia Dublan.

During the Revolution, Villa had no interest in attacking or causing the death of U.S. Army troops. Before the Agua Prieta fiasco, Villa was on friendly terms with Generals Scott and Pershing. General Scott spoke Spanish and throughout the Revolution he had met with Villa several times to discuss border issues and military tactics. Villa admired the military protocols and discipline displayed by the American soldiers.

The Aftermath

From a historical perspective, the skirmishes at Parral and Carrizal raise a number of interesting issues.

- The military order to pursue Villa was ambiguous to follow, either because it was issued so soon, within one day of the attack on Columbus, New Mexico, or because it was purposely prepared in an ambiguous manner. The order refers to the "Mexican band," meaning a group of bandits. Villa had been fighting for the Revolution for six years. At the time of the raid, he held the title of Brigadier General of the Army of the North. He had led military campaigns against Diaz, Orozco, Huerta, and Carranza, and was now in a legitimate conflict with Carranza over the true leadership of the nation. It appears that use of the word "bandit" was needed to justify the cost of the expedition and gain the support of the American public.

- After the Carrizal incident, President Wilson stated that Mexico did not have a formal government, implying that the nation was out of control. Yet, only a few months earlier in October of 1915, he formally recognized Carranza as the de facto President of Mexico. On the one hand he had affirmed Carranza was the right man to lead the nation, while on the other hand, he was now saying there was no true leader in Mexico. In between the lines one can clearly see that President Wilson's diplomacy had backfired when Carranza refused to support the expedition. Rather than President Wilson admitting his own shortcomings, it was more convenient to blame Carranza.

- When the expedition proved to be an embarrassment, President Wilson found it convenient to forget that he had been a willing participant in the life and death struggle between Carranza and Villa. Wilson had supported Carranza by recognizing him as the Primer Jefe, and by providing military trains to transport Carranza troops to travel to Agua Prieta, and by placing an arms embargo on Villa. All of this was intended for the forces of Villa to collapse, be captured, and eventually executed by Carranza.

- On his own initiative, Carranza had installed himself as the Primer Jefe. He had no more right to become the Primer Jefe than any of the other leaders of the Revolution, be it Villa, Zapata, Felipe Ángeles, or Alvaro Obregón. When he became Primer Jefe, he acted no differently than the usurper Huerta in assuming power without being properly elected by a democratic process. Moreover, it was Carranza who sabotaged the Aguascalientes Convention when he was voted out of office as the Primer Jefe. He stated to General Obregón that the Convention had no authority to elect a Provisional President (Eulalio Gutierrez). In addition, although by the time of the attack on Columbus, Villa had lost some crucial battles, he still commanded an army that was fighting for someone other than Carranza to be the recognized leader of the nation.

- The raid on Columbus occurred on March 9, and by March 15 General Pershing had entered Mexico with over 10,000 troops. In 1916, the technology did not exist to mobilize a large body of soldiers in one week. It is clear that the United States Government had preconceived plans to invade Mexico. The only question that remained was to find the right opportunity to justify an invasion of a sovereign nation. Villa was a revolutionary leader who had violated the sovereign rights of the U.S. and had committed crimes in doing so. Yet, there is no evidence that the U.S. made an effort to meet with Carranza to discuss military strategy to apprehend Villa. Essentially, Carranza was told to accept the fact that the U.S. was going to invade Mexico and he had no choice in the matter.

- The military orders issued to Pershing were to pursue and disband the "bandit," and the U.S. Army would withdraw after Carranza troops had taken over. These orders were flawed because they did not provide for Mexican property rights and safeguards of civilian life, or due process if prisoners were captured. Numerous times during the expedition, Pershing's invaded small villages, ransacked homes, and destroyed property. There is no evidence that the villagers were compensated by the U.S. for these damages. On the other hand, the residents of Columbus were compensated for the damages caused by the Villa raid. In the skirmishes in Parral and Carrizal, several Mexican soldiers were killed. This constitutes wrongful death because the Carranza troops were not the enemy.

This is particularly true in the Carrizal incident where it was clearly established that Captain Boyd instigated the incident. Perhaps the most grievous flaw of the expedition was what to do with Pancho Villa if he was captured? Was he going to be turned over to Carranza, who most assuredly would have him summarily executed, or were they going to take him to the U.S. and put him in prison? In which case, Villa would have been entitled to judicial hearing. All charges would have to be listed, including an articulation as to the laws that had been violated, and Villa would have been entitled to his own legal defense. Thus, President Wilson would have to provide evidence before a court of law, the necessity, justification, and ramifications of the expedition, including the use of military trains to defeat Villa at Agua Prieta.

Why weren't Captain Boyd and General Pershing charged with dereliction of duty concerning the loss of American and Mexican lives at Parral and Carrizal? At the time of the Carrizal incident, General Pershing was under strict military orders not to reconnoiter beyond his base at Colonia Dublan. Captain Boyd was on a patrol to determine the strength of Carranza troops at Villa Ahumada, in the east, which is in the opposite direction where Villa was hiding, in the west. Moreover, Boyd took deliberate action to engage Carranza, in spite of the fact he was requested twice to proceed no further. He was not truthful when he stated that he had orders to pass through Carrizal in search of an army deserter and bandits.

Justice for All

The 17 Villa soldiers that were captured in the Columbus raid were sent to prison in Deming, New Mexico. On August 17, 1917, the 17 Villa prisoners were charged with first degree murder for the deaths of eight civilians. To avoid being hanged, the 17 prisoners were advised to plead guilty to a lesser crime. They were lead to believe that if they pleaded guilty, they would only serve two to three years in prison. However, most of the prisoners were found guilty and sentenced from seventy to eighty years in State prison in Santa Fe, New Mexico. Guadalupe Chavez pleaded not guilty, the death sentence of José Rodriguez was commuted, Silvino Vargas had been pardoned, and Enrique Adame had escaped.

The main question that arises is why were the Villistas prosecuted by the State of New Mexico? Assuming they were guilty, theirs was a federal offense for having violated American territory. One day after the raid, the U.S. Government authorized an expedition to capture (and presumably bring to justice) the persons responsible for the raid. This implied the U.S. Government had assumed jurisdiction over the incident. Moreover, this was an international incident involving two countries. Thus, the applicable laws involved federal statutes, not state statutes. This distinction was well known to the State of New Mexico at the time of the trial, and yet the federal government made no effort to assert jurisdiction.

On the other hand, when the 24 Americans were taken prisoners at Carrizal, within days they were returned to the U.S. Had Carranza wanted to, he could have put the Americans on trial for the death of Mexican soldiers. The stated purpose of the expedition was to pursue Pancho Villa. There were no provisions in the military orders issued to Pershing to engage Carranza troops or citizens in a firefight. The death of Carranza soldiers was a blunder on the part the U.S. Army. On the other hand, when Carranza captured American troops, he accepted the fact that the troopers were just following orders and for this reason he returned them to the U.S. without delay.

Four years later, as matters turned out, on November 22, 1920, all the Villista prisoners that attacked Columbus were pardoned by Octaviano Larrazalo, the Governor of New Mexico. He pardoned them on the basis they were regular soldiers who were just following orders. Moreover, it was a known fact that many of the more recent Villa conscripts involved in the raid had been coerced in joining Villa; otherwise their families would be punished or executed. Even if they had known they were going to attack the U.S., they had no power to refuse to participate in the attack.

Although the prisoners captured at Columbus were pardoned, this was not the end of their fight for freedom. The American Legion organization initiated an effort to file new charges against the prisoner on the basis that the Governor of New Mexico did not have the power to grant a pardon. The prisoners were rearrested on murder charges. However, the New Mexico Supreme Court declared that the Governor did have the power to pardon. The prisoners were set free and returned to Mexico in February, 1918.

During the pursuit by Pershing in Mexico, a second group of 25 Villistas had been captured and were sent to New Mexico for trial. However, by this time the flames of prejudice and revenge from the first trial had subsided. The 25 prisoners were found not guilty on the grounds that they were regular soldiers following orders, which is exactly the conclusion reached by Carranza 10 months earlier regarding the Carrizal skirmish.

It is ironic that in both trials it was concluded the prisoners that attacked Columbus were soldiers who were following orders. The key word here is "soldiers," and yet when President Wilson authorized the military expedition he used the word "bandit."

The savage treatment of the Villistas killed in the raid is another tragic example of prejudice and vengeance contrary to human decency. The Villistas that were killed in the exchange of gun fire were stacked and soaked with kerosene and set aflame. All that remained were the charred bodies. As a war trophy, some

American troops and civilians posed for pictures with the charred bodies. The U.S. Army made no effort to identify the dead Villa soldiers so that their next of kin could be notified, nor did they make an effort to conduct a proper burial at the cemetery in Columbus, or to return the bodies to their families in Mexico.

Failure to capture Pancho Villa

When General Pershing pursued Villa, he had the services of the best military minds and a powerful military force under his command. He had a well-equipped army that included an experienced mounted cavalry, mobile truck transportation, and airplanes for reconnaissance. Within one week of the attack he moved quickly to deploy his troops. He enlisted Americans living in Mexico that spoke Spanish as scouts and recruited Apache Indians as elite trackers. Pershing had taken advantage of the vast resources that were made available for the expedition, except for one element of utmost consideration; he ignored the fact that Pancho Villa was the foremost guerrilla warrior of the Revolution.

Pershing's tactics were to send out numerous patrols a few miles apart in different directions to locate Villa's ever-changing hideout. Pershing assumed that Villa could not gain much distance because he would have to stop to rest the horses, find food, and replenish his supplies. And of course, all of this was true because Villa's forces were depleted even before he attacked Columbus. Pershing was calculating what Villa might do, instead of what Villa could do. That is, Villa might try stopping and hiding tactics until he put some distance between his Villistas and Pershing's forces. That way he would gain time and distance. From a military perspective, Pershing should have calculated what Villa could do, that is, Villa would be heading for Parral, Chihuahua. Pershing was a veteran of military tactics and he should have calculated that Villa would work his way to Parral (Villa's home base), as fast as possible. Parral was a stronghold for Villa and a place where he had fought several battles for the Revolution. He had excellent knowledge of the terrain, and as a Robin Hood, he had provided money and assistance to many of the campesinos. Based on these factors, Pershing, upon entering Mexico, should have sent a force of perhaps 1,000 men immediately to Parral to seal off Villa's escape route to the South.

General Pershing was expected to capture Villa, since he had been provided resources in men and material to achieve his military objective (according to U.S. Army military doctrine) General Pershing had several advantages:

- A clear strategic objective – capture Pancho Villa

- Was provided all the necessary military resources to bring about the capture of Pancho Villa.

- He was authorized the use of Spanish Speaking scouts, as well as several Apache Indians as trackers.

- He had the necessary funds to purchase intelligence. In addition, he had the cooperation of several Americans who owned large land and had business holdings.

- More importantly, he had an "end-game," that is to capture Villa as soon as possible and return to the United States with a clear victory.

Although General Pershing was a West Point graduate and the veteran of several military campaigns, he was not able capture Villa because he did not employ the appropriate strategy for capturing the most elusive guerilla fighter of the Revolution. In the annals of the American Army, few, if any, American General has been provided with 10,000 soldiers for the express purpose of capturing one individual target.

Villa had spent sixteen years in the mountains of Chihuahua and Durango as a fugitive and had avoided capture through cunning and instinct. Having been shot at and nearly captured several times, he had learned the lessons of survival well. If Villa escaped into the mountains, he would have been captured when his horses tired and food supplies ran out. If he escaped near larger villages, he would have been engaged by Carranza or Pershing troops. Had Pershing immediately deployed forces to Parral, he would have been pursuing Villa from north and south in a pincer movement towards the middle or near the village of Namiquipa. Instead, Pershing wrongfully assumed he could catch Villa while he was on the run, something that no adversary had been able to accomplish for twenty years.

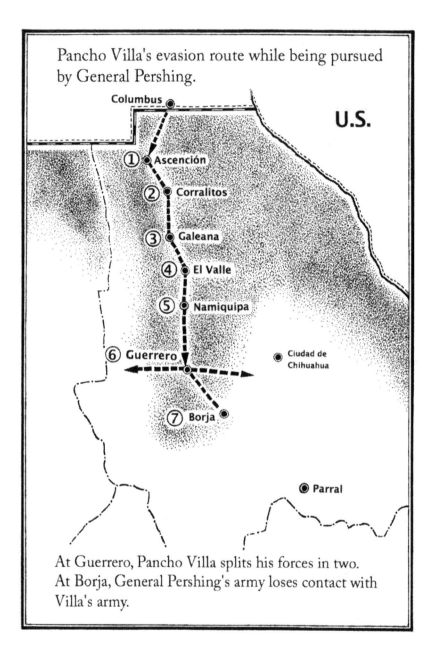

Pancho Villa's evasion route while being pursued by General Pershing.

At Guerrero, Pancho Villa splits his forces in two. At Borja, General Pershing's army loses contact with Villa's army.

Part Three – The Undeclared War against Mexico

Events leading to Intervention and Occupation of Mexico

During his Presidency, President Wilson intervened with military force in the affairs of Mexico on at least four occasions: On April 9, 1914, President Wilson ordered a Naval Blockade of the Port of Tampico, in the State of Tamaulipas; on April 21, 1914, he ordered the occupation of the Port of Veracruz, in the State of Veracruz; on October 10, 1915, he authorized the transport of the Mexican Army on U.S. railroads to engage Pancho Villa at Agua Prieta, Sonora; and on March 16, 1916, he ordered General Pershing to enter Mexico to capture Pancho Villa.[7]

It is important to note that these military initiatives were taken against Mexico when a state of war did not exist between the two countries. Some may argue the initiatives were necessary to protect U.S. interests and honor, when in reality U.S. interests and honor were not at stake. The U.S. military acts of intervention and occupation are indisputable and by any reasonable interpretation constitute military aggression that brought the U.S. to the brink of war against a weaker nation.

---

[7] In addition, during the period of the Mexican Revolution, President Wilson also authorized the occupation of Nicaragua in June 1911 and the Dominican Republic in May 1916.

Chapter XIII. "Protectorate Nation" Status

In the preface of this book, *Viva Villa*, the authors offer the theory that if General Pancho Villa had been captured, the United States would have gained control of the five northern Mexican states of Sonora, Chihuahua, Coahuila, Nuevo Leon, and Tamaulipas. This thesis is driven by the following considerations: (1) The United States' history of occupation; (2) Invasion by General Pershing; (3) Deceptive military orders issued to General Pershing; (4) War plans by the United States to invade Mexico; (5) Arbitrary entry by the United States into Mexico; (6) The specter of secret military orders; and (7) Protectorate nation history of the United States.

(1) The United States' History of Occupation

Blockade of the Port of Tampico

On April 9, 1914, American naval ships were sent to the Port of Tampico, presumably to protect American lives and business oil interests; however, the real purpose was to intimidate General Huerta into resigning his Presidency. While at the Port of Tampico, nine sailors landed on a whale boat, flying the American flag, to collect fuel supplies. As soon as they arrived, the sailors were detained by the Mexican Army for interrogation. Within one hour of being detained the Americans were allowed to return to their ship. The Commander of the American Fleet, Admiral Henry Mayo became upset because he believed that American honor had been disrespected and the American flag had been insulted. Admiral Mayo demanded an apology from the Mexican Government; a court martial for the arresting officer, and a 21-naval gun salute. When the matter was brought to the attention of General Huerta, he agreed to provide a written apology and

165

convene a court martial, but he refused to provide the 21-gun salute, unless Admiral Mayo reciprocated and returned the same salute. Admiral Mayo insisted that he must receive a naval salute without reciprocity. General Huerta refused the unilateral demand and requested the matter be submitted for international arbitration.

President Wilson did not acknowledge General Huerta's request for arbitration, instead he decided to ask Congress to require Mexico to comply with the request for a 21-gun salute. General Huerta was given an ultimatum to comply, or else the U.S. would take military action against Mexico. General Huerta, who had wrongfully assumed the Presidency of Mexico, refused for two reasons; since President Wilson had not recognized General Huerta as the legitimate government of Mexico, why should he now recognize President Wilson; and what if General Huerta fired the salute and the Americans decided not to return the same? General Huerta believed that he needed a reciprocal salute in order to maintain his prestige with the Mexican people. Based on the refusal by General Huerta to comply with the American request, President Wilson obtained approval of the U.S. Congress to blockade the Ports of Tampico and Veracruz.

Occupation of the Port of Veracruz

Within a few days after the Tampico affair, President Wilson learned the Germany ship *Ypiranga* was on its way to Mexico to deliver a large shipment of arms for General Huerta. Since President Wilson was so intent on removing General Huerta from the Presidency, he took immediate action to prevent the *Ypiranga* from arriving at the Port of Veracruz.

On April 21, 1914, the U.S. Atlantic Fleet, consisting of 25 war ships, including the largest battleships in the U.S. Navy, entered Mexican waters at Veracruz to land 3,500 sailors and marines. The battleships USS Florida and USS Utah were stationed outside of Veracruz. As the USS Prairie, San Francisco, and Chester entered Veracruz, the naval cadets at the Mexican Naval Academy opened fire against the Americans. The U.S. Navy responded by pulverizing the Mexican Naval Academy. The naval cadets with small cannon and rifle fire were no match for the 14" naval guns on the U.S. Battleships that could destroy a target at a distance of 10-15 miles.

United States Navy Battleship Florida

The USS Florida was assigned to occupy the Port of Veracruz to intimidate Gen. Huerta into resigning his Presidency. The USS Florida had orders to intercept the German Ship *Ypiranga* when it arrived at Veracruz, to prevent the delivery of munitions from Germany for General Huerta.

United States Navy Battleship Utah

The USS Utah was assigned to guard American interests at the Port of Tampico in 1913. When U.S. sailors went ashore to collect some needed fuel, they were detained and released to return to their ship within one hour by the Mexican Navy. Nonetheless, Admiral Henry B. Mayo demanded that the Mexican Navy provide the USS Utah with a 21-naval gun salute, a written apology, and fly the American flag. The Mexican Navy refused.

The naval blockade was followed by a landing of 5,000 U.S. Army troops under the command of General Fredrick Funston, who took full control of the Port of Veracruz and flew the American flag for seven months, until the blockade was lifted on November 23, 1914. Nineteen American sailors and marines were killed; seventy-one were wounded; while over three hundred Mexicans were killed, including several Mexican naval cadets.

President Wilson had three objectives in ordering the naval blockade: intimidate General Huerta into resigning his Presidency, prevent the shipment of German arms and munitions from reaching General Huerta, and protect American oil deposits at a time when ships from the U.S. and Great Britain were converting from coal consumption to oil consumption. The bombardment of Veracruz was tantamount to an act of war, and the occupation of Veracruz constituted an abuse of power by President Wilson when you consider that Mexico's Navy was practically non-existent. In addition, Mexico had no military plans for destroying the oil fields because Mexico needed the revenues from the sale of oil to the U.S. to support the cost of the Revolution. More importantly, the leaders of the Revolution did not need the assistance of President Wilson to topple General Huerta. By April 1914, Carranza, Obregon, Zapata, and Villa were unified in a total effort to remove General Huerta from office. In addition, by this time, General Felipe Angeles had devised a brilliant military plan to defeat General Huerta's Federal Army in a pincer movement from the north and south. The combined forces of the Armies of the Revolution were on the march with perhaps over 60,000 troops, compared to 15,000 troops that were deployed to remove President Porfirio Diaz in 1911. General Huerta's federal army was not large, nor strong enough to defeat the Armies of the Revolution (moreover, Pancho Villa had already declared that he would avenge the death of Madero and Abraham Gonzalez, his two idols of the Revolution). Thus, it would be only a matter of a few months before General Huerta would be dislodged from Mexico City. As matters turned out, General Huerta was forced to resign on July 15, 1914, a mere fifteen months after wrongfully assuming the Presidency of Mexico.

Also, it is important to note that President Wilson never received the 21-naval gun salute he demanded, the *Ypiranga* landed only a few miles from Veracruz and delivered its cargo for General Huerta, and the U.S. troops that occupied Veracruz served no purpose other than to protect American oil interest.

169

Another unsavory outcome of the occupation of Veracruz was the excessive number of Medal of Honor (MOH) commendations awarded to the sailors and marines for a two day battle. According to military records, 52 Medals of Honor were awarded to 28 Marines, and 24 Navy personnel. This represents an inordinate amount of MOH awarded for a two day battle, particularly, when you consider that 119 MOH were awarded during World War I, 136 during the four-year Korean War, 465 during WW II, and 247 awarded during the eight-year Vietnam War. Although some of the marines and sailors earned high honors for bravery, it is dubious that all 52 met the high standards for awarding the MOH. For example, of the 52 recipients: 17 were naval officers who were not in the line of fire because they had never left their ship nor entered a combat zone. Most of the commendations were awarded for bravery under fire, but not necessarily due to the destruction of the enemy while under intense battle conditions. One recipient, Marine Corp Lieutenant Smedley Butler (who later entered Mexico City as a spy to evaluate the possible full occupation of Mexico), offered to return his MOH because he did not believe he had earned the commendation. He was instructed by the U.S. Navy to accept the MOH and to wear it in public.

Side Note:

During World War II, Mr. Ralph Hernandez, father of Robert B. Hernandez (one of the authors) served with the U.S. Navy on a landing ship (LSM 46) in the Pacific war zone. The LSM, destined for combat in the Pacific, traveled from Galveston, Texas to the Pacific Ocean via the Panama Canal. While crossing the Pacific Ocean they ran into a violent typhoon that caused substantial damage to the ship. The damage was such that it was necessary find a safe harbor at Salina Cruz, Oaxaca, Mexico. It was the intention of the American Captain to disembark, re-supply the ship, and communicate with the U.S. Fleet in San Diego. When the ship arrived at Salina Cruz, the American Captain designated Hernandez to be the interpreter because he spoke Spanish. The LSM was met by the Harbor Pilot, but when the Harbor Pilot and the Harbor Master returned, the Harbor Master made some comments that Hernandez could not understand. The Captain quickly snapped at Hernandez and asked, "What the hell is going on here, Hernandez. I thought you could speak Spanish." Hernandez replied, "Yes I do, but this fellow is speaking an Indian dialect." (Evidently Zapotec since it is the dialect of that region of Oaxaca.)

Mr. Hernandez overheard the Harbor pilot implore the Harbor Master to speak Spanish, but the Harbor Master uttered an insult in Spanish about the Americans. Mr. Hernandez strongly reminded the Harbor Master that this was an official request from the U.S. Navy. After a pause, the Harbor Master responded back with fluent Spanish, in a more polite and attentive tone, indicating Mr. Hernandez should inform his Captain that the American ship would have to stay in place for one day until he contacted the Mexican Navy.

The next day a small contingent of Mexican naval staff arrived and requested permission to come on board. The Mexican naval officer, who was impeccably dressed in navy whites, granted the American flag a smart salute.

After some discussion it was agreed the LSM would enter the harbor and disembark. Before entering the harbor, the controls for adjusting speed were taped and the radio was disabled by the Mexican Navy.

The LSM 46 stayed at Salina Cruz two weeks before it was towed to San Diego for repairs.

Hernandez was quite proud to have used his Spanish to resolve the issues raised in the discussions. He was quite impressed with the spit and polish on the part of the Mexican Navy and their ability to stand fast in observing proper protocols between the two countries.

On the way to Iwo Jima, LSM 46 stopped at Ullthi, in Caroline Islands, to load U.S. Marines, tanks, and war supplies. On the second day in the battle zone, the LSM received heavy mortar fire that damaged the ship and killed three sailors and wounded seventeen. Due to the battle damage, the ship had to return to San Diego for major repairs. The stay in San Diego enabled the ship to avoid the deadly Kamikaze attacks at the Battle of Okinawa only a few months later.

Transportation of the Mexican Army on United States Railroad System

In October 1915, President Wilson authorized the transportation of 5,000 Mexican Army troops from Eagle Pass, Texas, to Douglas, Arizona. While this did not constitute an occupation, the incident was an act of war and a violation of international law governing the rights of a sovereign nation. The Mexican Army was transported over U.S. soil, and U.S. railways to arrive at Douglas,

Arizona, in time to engage Pancho Villa in the battle for the City of Agua Prieta, in the State of Sonora. When the Mexican Army arrived at Douglas, they simply disembarked and walked across the border to augment Carranza troops preparing to defend Agua Prieta (Douglas and Agua Prieta are separated by a city street). When Pancho Villa attacked Agua Prieta, he was met by 6,500 Carranza troops instead of the 1,500 he expected. The U.S. Army also provided Carranza troops with heavy-duty search lights that were reportedly powered by the City of Douglas, knowing that Villa always attacked at dawn. The next day, Villas' forces were repulsed, and he had to retreat to the State of Chihuahua to regroup his tattered army.

In addition to transporting the Mexican Army, the U.S. Army also deployed 7,500 American soldiers at Douglas under the command of General Fredrick Funston, the Commander for American forces along the U.S.—Mexico Border. Given the high rank of General Funston, it is reasonable to conclude he was present to give the order to attack Pancho Villa's Army, in the event Carranza's troops were overpowered. Also, the presence of American troops could easily trigger a firefight between the U.S. Army and Pancho Villa should the U.S. Army sustain casualties due to errant rifle fire from Pancho Villa or Carranza soldiers.

Note: More than once Carranza troops fired bullets on the American side of the border to turn the U.S. Army against Villa.

(2) The Invasion by General Pershing

After the attack on Columbus, New Mexico on March 9, 1916, many Americans demanded retribution be taken to crush Pancho Villa. In response to the American outcry for war, the U.S. Army War College prepared war plans for the invasion of Mexico (War Plan Green). The War College is charged with preparing contingency war plans against any number of countries. Under War Plan Green, President Wilson opted for a military force of 10,000 that became known as the Punitive Expedition. He believed that such an expedition would capture Pancho Villa and satisfy the demands of Americans who wanted all-out war with Mexico. It would also redeem the honor of the U.S.; and it would provide personal retribution against Pancho Villa for having invaded the U.S. (See map at end of chapter.)

The authors of the book, *Viva Villa*, believe that sending 10,000 American Cavalry Troops over 500 miles into the interior of Mexico represented an excessive show of force, and in effect constituted an act of war. According to American military reports, Villa had 350 Villistas when he attacked Columbus. By the time he re-entered Mexico, only 250 Villistas remained, having lost 100 men during the attack and escape from the Columbus raid. Moreover, at the time of the Columbus raid, Villa did not constitute a major military force. His forces had been depleted in earlier engagements when he was soundly defeated in the cities of Celaya, Leon, and Agua Prieta. His munitions were low because President Wilson had placed an embargo on weapons, Villa could not obtain munitions unless he paid gun runners from the United States, and his army was completely exhausted and near starvation. In addition, American military intelligence had reports that the Villistas that attacked Columbus included a large number of young teenagers without guerilla warfare experience. Some of the Villistas in the Columbus raid were as young as fifteen and sixteen, while others, who had been forced to join Villa by threatening their families, had no knowledge that Villa was going to attack Columbus, and, thus, were likely to leave Villa as soon as they returned to Mexico.

Another consideration is the fact that Villa was being

aggressively pursued by General Alvaro Obregón, his nemesis from the battle for Celaya. It was only a question of time before General Obregón would encircle Villa. Obregón's army was large, well equipped, and intent on capturing Villa to end the Revolution once and for all. Undoubtedly, Obregón still remembered Villa when he lost his right arm to Villa's artillery in the battle for Leon, Guanajuato, or perhaps the time Obregón was almost placed before a firing squad by Villa in 1914, when he had gone to Chihuahua City to smooth out problems between Carranza and Villa. Unknown to Obregón, a plan was underway to assassinate Villa. Quite naturally, Villa assumed that Obregón was in charge of the assassination plot and ordered that Obregón be executed. However, Obregón was able to plead a rational argument that he had not been sent to conduct an assassination. Villa accepted Obregón's explanation and allowed him to return to Carranza, but Obregón never forgot how close he came to being placed on the paredon (against the firing wall).

The swiftness with which the Pershing Expedition was organized is suspect and gives doubt as to the U.S. ultimate objective for invading Mexico. The Columbus raid occurred on March 9, and by March 16, over 10,000 American troops had been mobilized, all within seven days. The military mobilization of a large army involved complicated logistics requiring time to organize. Thus, it is clear the U.S. military had prepared war plans for the invasion of Mexico, even before the incident occurred at Columbus, New Mexico. In view of the rapid deployment and the size of the military force, one can only conclude that the U.S. was, in effect, waiting for the appropriate border incident to initiate military action against Mexico. There is no other satisfactory explanation.

Engagements in Parral and Carrizal, Chihuahua

In April, 1916, the American Cavalry engaged Carranza troops at Parral, and in June, at Carrizal, Chihuahua. That such incidents would occur was forecast by the War College Division when it reviewed the purpose of the Punitive Expedition. The War College Division had warned that an expedition focused on the capture of one individual, Pancho Villa, involved certain military risks. The warning materialized when the American cavalry engaged Carranza troops, instead of the cavalry of Pancho Villa, at Parral and Carrizal. These two military incidents brought the U.S. to the brink of war with Mexico.

Firefight at Parral, Chihuahua: The first military incident occurred on April 12, 1916, when Major Frank Tompkins sought passage through the town of Parral but was halted by the local Mexican commander. When the Americans began to retreat, someone fired a rifle, and soon a firefight was started between American and Mexican troops. Three Americans and eight Mexicans soldiers were killed in the exchange of gunfire.

After the military action at Parral, General Pershing proposed that the war effort be escalated and requested approval from the War Department to occupy and seize all of the railroads in the State of Chihuahua, and occupy Chihuahua City. His request was denied. On April 12, higher level American military officials also began to seriously consider war with Mexico. General Hugh Scott, Army Chief of Staff, recommended to President Wilson that the National Guard be activated and placed along the border for deployment as necessary. Accordingly, on May 9, 1916, Secretary of War Newton Baker authorized National Guard troops to be deployed along the border in the states of Arizona, New Mexico, and Texas.

Firefight at Carrizal, Chihuahua: The second military incident occurred on June 21, 1916, at Carrizal, when a U.S.

Cavalry Detachment under the command of Captain Charles T. Boyd engaged Mexican soldiers at the small village of Carrizal, located near the main highway to Chihuahua City. In the ensuing engagement, twelve American soldiers were killed, twelve were wounded, and twenty-four were captured; forty-two Mexicans were killed and fifty-one were wounded.

Had the Mexican commander made a determined effort to destroy the American troops, the incident at Carrizal could have easily turned into another Little Big Horn, where Colonel George C. Custer's cavalry of 150 was decimated on June 25, 1876, by the Sioux Indian Nation. The events were similar in that both Captain Boyd and Colonel Custer were faced with a superior force, were too far away from reinforcements, were not familiar with the terrain, and were faced by an enemy with deep resentment. In addition, both Colonel Custer and Captain Boyd had disobeyed orders and were known to be hot heads.

When the incident was investigated, it was determined that Captain Boyd was at fault for attempting to pass through Carrizal without proper authority. According to Bruce Johnson, noted historian on Woodrow Wilson, "Boyd was spoiling for a fight." Immediately following the Carrizal incident, General Funston, in charge of the border area, was ordered to seize all border bridges in preparations for invading Mexico.

The incident at Carrizal shook President Wilson deeply. His determination to avoid war with Mexico fell apart, and quick action was needed to prevent full escalation leading to war between the two countries.

Diplomatic Developments

Letter by Candido Aguilar, Secretary of Foreign Affairs: A letter sent by Secretary Aguilar contributed to the uneasiness of relations with Mexico. On May 22, 1916, the Mexican Secretary for

Foreign Affairs, sent American Secretary of State Lansing a scathing letter stating that the expedition had to be withdrawn. He indicated that the Americans (Punitive Expedition) were heavy handed, they were the intruders, and they should leave Mexico as soon as possible. Secretary Lansing replied that the U.S. would stay in Mexico until it believed it had met the objective of the Punitive Expedition, meaning until they had captured Pancho Villa.

Warning by General Trevino

The second development occurred on June 16, when Mexican General Jacinto Trevino sent General Pershing an official communiqué that the American Army could not move any further south than Parral, Chihuahua. General Trevino warned that if General Pershing attempted to move further south or turned east or west, he would use military force to stop any further penetration of Mexican territory, in other words, General Pershing should make plans to return to the U.S. General Pershing answered that the American Government had not altered his plans regarding his military movements, nor the deployment of his troops. He stated to the Mexican Commander that he would purse Pancho Villa until he was captured and any military consequences would be the responsibility of General Trevino.

Release of Prisoners

On June 28, 1916, Carranza ordered that the twenty-four Americans captured at Carrizal be returned to the U.S. This clearly indicated that Carranza did not want war with the U.S. Carranza could have easily held a trial for the captured Americans for having killed Mexican Constitutionalist soldiers. Carranza would have been on sound legal grounds if he argued that the American Army objective was to capture Pancho Villa, not to engage soldiers of the Mexican Army.

The High Commission: In July, 1916, President Wilson initiated the establishment of a "Joint High Commission" to investigate the turmoil between Mexico and the U.S. The High Commission met at various times and locations, such as New Jersey, Connecticut, and Philadelphia, fifty-four times in four months. The highlight of the High Commission was to recommend that the Punitive Expedition be withdrawn from Mexico, but its implementation was delayed because the parties could not agree on a specific timetable for withdrawal. The Mexican representatives wanted a specific timeline. The Americans did not want to provide a specific timeline for fear that "undisciplined" Carranza troops would attack the Americans while they retreated. The American rationale does not stand the test of good faith, when you consider that the purpose of the High Commission was to arrive at a mutually acceptable and workable solution for the withdrawal of the Punitive Expedition. Moreover, only six months earlier President Wilson had recognized Carranza as the de facto leader of Mexico, indicating he was trustworthy regarding protocols between the two nations.

(3) Deceptive Military Orders issued to General Pershing

The military orders issued to General Pershing were deceptive regarding the true purpose of the expedition. The orders were as follows:

> "You will promptly organize an adequate military force of troops under the command of Brigadier General Pershing and will direct him to proceed promptly across the border in Pursuit of the *Mexican band* [italics by the author] which attacked the town of Columbus ... These troops will be withdrawn to American territory as soon as the de facto government of Mexico is able to

relieve them of this work. In any event the work of these troops will be regarded as finished as soon as *Villa band* [italics by the author], or bands are known to be broken up ...."

Note: In the above military orders, "Mexican band" and "Villa band" imply that Pancho Villa's men were a bandit group. By the time the Punitive Expedition entered Mexico, Pancho Villa was fully engaged in the revolution against Carranza. Moreover, Villa had the rank of Brigadier General when he was promoted by President Francisco Madero. The military orders could have stated "revolutionary group," "insurgents," or "the Conventionist's Army."

On March 9, 1916, when the attack occurred on Columbus, it may have been convenient for President Wilson to call Pancho Villa a bandit. This would certainly provide proper patriotic appeal for the American people to support the expedition and redeem the honor of the U.S. What is overlooked is the fact that only six months earlier, President Wilson could have recognized either Pancho Villa or Carranza as the de facto President of Mexico. For political reasons, President Wilson chose to recognize Carranza, and not Villa. In other words, six months earlier Pancho Villa was not considered a "bandit."

Up until the time that Carranza was recognized as the de facto leader, Villa and Carranza had been involved in a death struggle for the leadership of Mexico. By any reasonable definition, Pancho Villa was not a bandit. In 1910, when he joined the Revolution, Villa was made a Captain and later promoted to Colonel. In 1912, when he was reactivated for military duty to fight Pascual Orozco he was made a Brigadier General under the authority of President Francisco Madero. Moreover, during the campaigns to remove Porfirio Diaz and Victoriano Huerta, Villa's army of 15,000 to 20,000 were always larger than that of Carranza.

It is a historical fact that Villa had his rank as general assigned to him by Madero, the legally constituted President of Mexico. After Madero was assassinated in 1913, neither Villa nor Carranza had any constitutional authority to designate what rank should be assigned to any of the Revolutionaries. Carranza's Plan of Guadalupe was a localized plan that emanated from his home state of Coahuila as a temporary measure until General Huerta could be removed from office.

Carranza was mainly responsible for the negative propaganda attributed to Villa as a bandit and an unsavory person when he paid American journalists to write defamatory articles about Villa. He also retained the services of Kenneth Cole, Washington DC lobbyist[8], to promote his image in the U.S. During the 1910-1913 period of the Revolution, Villa was held in high esteem by the Revolutionaries, American press, and the American military. It was not until after the Convention of Aguascalientes in October 1914, that Carranza paid journalists in Mexico and the U.S. to defame Villa. At the Aguascalientes Convention, Carranza had been asked to resign as Primer Jefe. He refused to resign, and an all-out war ensued between Villa and Carranza. By defaming Villa, Carranza could secure the financial and economic support he needed from President Wilson. Moreover, all generals of the Revolution were guilty of confiscating property, imposing ransom, hanging and executing prisoners. Some generals were guilty of more crimes than others. The only exception was General Felipe Ángeles, who went out of his way to ensure that prisoners were not executed.

------

[8] Romantic Tragedies of Mexico, 1956, Merl Burke Cole, The Christopher Publishing House, Boston U.S.A.

Execution of prisoners was common; hanging of prisoners was less common. However, all leaders of the Revolution conducted hangings as a warning to the enemy. Depicted is a hanging conducted by Carranza soldiers

When the U.S. Army entered Mexico in pursuit of Pancho Villa, no charges were presented to the Government of Mexico regarding any violations of the laws of the U.S. Since no formal charges were filed against Villa by the U.S., what then was the justification to enter Mexico against the will of the people and the de facto government? Moreover, of the 17 Villa soldiers that were captured during the Columbus raid, after two trials, all were ultimately found innocent on the basis that they were soldiers following orders. So how is it conceivable for a "bandit" to be in charge of "soldiers" where it was established they were only following military orders?

War Plan Green

(4) War Plans by the United States to invade Mexico

Following the demand for a 21-naval gun salute at the Port of Tampico, and the naval occupation of the Port of Veracruz in 1914, the United States military believed there was a possibility of war with Mexico. In addition, Venustiano Carranza, who had become Primer Jefe, warned President Wilson that American troops were not welcome in Mexico. In anticipation of war, the Army War College Division, which is responsible for planning military strategy, developed war plans indicating that 246,000 troops would be needed if the U.S. went to war with Mexico.

On March 4, 1916, only five days before the raid on Columbus, the War College Division updated its 1914 war plans for invading Mexico. Their assessment was that the continuing border incidents could only be alleviated by a full military occupation of Mexico, followed by a period of pacification. The War College Division did not recommend a limited military objective, such as the Punitive Expedition to enter Mexico to capture one person. They believed that such a large force involved too many military risks if the objective was limited to one person. (General Hugh Scott, U.S. Army Chief of Staff.)

In addition, the Mexican Secretary of Foreign Affairs, Candido Aguilar, on June 16, 1916, sent a letter to the U.S. Government to remove American troops from Mexico. General Scott again ordered that the War Plans for invading Mexico be updated. The new military objective was to engage the Mexican Army if it attempted to impede the Punitive Expedition. The War College Division developed the following plan: protect the border; set up an invasion route along the axis of each railroad line leading into the heart of Mexico; take over the railroads; manage, repair and build bridges for the railroads; establish communications lines; start a major highway from Columbus to Namiquipa, Chihuahua (about 250 miles from Columbus); and assign 1,600 new troops to the border.

To implement the anticipated invasion, army strength would be augmented to include 30,000 troops to depart from Brownsville, Texas under General Funston; 30,000 from El Paso, Texas under General Pershing; 10,000 from Nogales, Arizona under General Sage; and 30,000 for border security. In addition, the U.S. Navy would sail with 10,000 troops towards Tampico and Veracruz. This part of the plan was designed to draw Carranza's army south, away from the intended invasion route. The diversionary tactic of sending troops to Veracruz was an excellent piece of planning when you consider that Veracruz had been occupied by U.S. Marines for seven months in 1914, only two years earlier. In addition, military minds were well aware that the route from Veracruz to Mexico City is the traditional route for the occupation of Mexico: Hernan Cortes, in 1519, used it when conquering the Mexica Empire, and General Zachary Scott used it in 1846 in the war with Mexico, the French Army (Maximilian and Carlotta) used it in 1861, when it invaded Mexico.

(5) Arbitrary Entry by the United States into Mexico

When the Punitive Expedition entered Mexico, it did not have the approval of Primer Jefe Carranza. The U.S. had made several diplomatic attempts to convince Carranza to agree to the insertion of the Punitive Expedition, but Carranza was steadfast in his belief that the U.S. military should not be invading Mexico.

When all diplomatic attempts failed, Carranza then initiated a "Hot Pursuit" agreement. Carranza wanted to have the same opportunity for the Mexican Army to pursue American bandits who invaded Mexico and returned to the U.S. to seek refuge. Carranza believed that if a Hot Pursuit agreement was adopted, he could save face by telling the Mexican people that justice worked both ways, thus it was acceptable for the Punitive Expedition to enter Mexico to chase Pancho Villa. The Americans did not want the agreement because it would give Mexico too much authority over American affairs along the border. Eventfully, the agreement was signed because the U.S. believed that it was in their best interest to sign the agreement in order to allay the negative criticism that was emerging from other Latin American countries that were closely monitoring the events that led to the Punitive Expedition.

The crucial point to consider is that the agreement was arrived at after the Punitive Expedition had already entered Mexico. In view of this fact, Carranza continued to hold that the Americans should leave Mexico. The U.S., on the other hand, conveniently chose to believe they had a gentlemen's agreement with Carranza to pursue Villa. It is indisputable that the U.S. entered Mexico in an arbitrary manner and without the approval of Mexico. President Wilson failed to understand that he was dictating American policy and imposing its military might on the internal affairs of a foreign country. The arbitrary entry into Mexico only served to build resentment against the U.S., and it gave Pancho Villa a second life. Within weeks Villa reestablished his army, captured several cities in the State of Chihuahua, and went on the offensive against Carranza. In the meantime, General Pershing, having caused political upheaval regarding the unwarranted military skirmishes at Parral and Carrizal, remained dormant at his military base at Colonia Dublan, near Columbus, New Mexico.

(6) The Specter of Secret Military Orders

Whenever a country is considering occupation of a foreign country under false pretenses, the first order of business is to prepare secret orders to gain a military advantage. Secret military orders, designated "Classified" to preclude access by the American public, have been used by the U.S. in the past. The military orders given to General Pershing had a very specific military objective: capture Pancho Villa. When the proposed military orders were reviewed by the staff of the War College, the experts in military planning emphatically stated that military orders specifying one person were not suitable for the purpose of the punitive expedition. President Wilson rejected the War

College recommendation that the name, Pancho Villa be deleted.

Since General Pershing was not given typical broad military orders through his chain of command, this raises the specter that perhaps he was given secret military orders by President Wilson, perhaps written, but mostly likely verbal. The size of the military expedition, 10,000 men, certainly indicates that the expedition may have involved other military objectives. Perhaps General Pershing had secret orders to occupy the City of Zacatecas after he captured Pancho Villa. The City of Zacatecas is of strategic importance as well as the gateway to Mexico City, via Mexico's railroad system. The Mexican railroad system was built under the Diaz regime by American companies. Thus, if General Pershing requested the plans for the railroad system, they would undoubtedly be made available to him. Moreover, throughout the Revolution, military commanders fought ferociously to defend or capture Zacatecas, knowing that its capture would ensure rapid deployment to Mexico City. (See end of chapter for Theoretical Orders.)

The potential that General Pershing was given secret orders is not a new concept in American military affairs. Secret orders have been used in the past by the U.S. Some historians have indicated that secret orders were issued to General Andrew Jackson in 1817 when he was ordered to conquer the Seminole Indians, and to Captain John C. Fremont during the war with Mexico in 1846.

In 1817, General Andrew Jackson was ordered by President Monroe to the Florida territory to quell the Seminole Indians who had been attacking American settlers. Jackson's military objective was limited to pacifying the Seminole Indians so that American settlers could travel safely in the Florida Territory. Jackson exceeded his orders when he conquered all of Florida and completely subjugated the Seminoles. Some historians allege that

Jackson had secret orders from President Monroe to occupy all of Florida, but this could not be made public because President Monroe did not want war with Spain, and he feared a backlash from the American public. Since General Jackson occupied all of Florida, measures were taken by Congress to censure him for having exceeded his military orders. However, since everybody loves a winner, the censure did not prevail when it was determined that General Jackson acted in the best interest of the United States.

In the summer of 1832, Captain John C. Fremont was sent by President Tyler on a geographic expedition to map the Oregon Territory. President Tyler was an avowed expansionist and was concerned that the Russian Government was making plans for the annexation of California by securing the Presidios of Monterey and San Francisco. The Fremont expedition included soldiers, map makers, and scouts. The expedition was successful and opened the way for more westward expansion. However, on Jun 1, 1845, just before the start of war with Mexico, Fremont was sent to California a second time with 62 soldiers, ostensibly on another geographic expedition, but this time the expedition included expert rifle shooters, as well as several artillery pieces. When Captain Fremont arrived in California, it became common knowledge that he was sent to incite a rebellion against the Mexican Government and was asked to leave California by General Castro.

As he was leaving California, he was intercepted by Lieutenant Archibald Gillespie, who was disguised as a merchant. Some historians allege that Gillispie gave Fremont secret orders to return to California to initiate a revolt against the Mexican Government by the California Bear Flaggers. In the Salinas Valley, Fremont established an outpost on Gavilan Peak, where he raised the American flag and declared that California now belonged to the United States.

(7) Protectorate Nation History of the United States

For several years, the U.S. had developed an inclination for dominating other countries by imposing the doctrine of Protectorate Nation. The U.S. would land a military force and assume full control of the country until the U.S. believed there was sufficient political and economic stability in the affected nation.

Many Americans do not believe that the U.S. has been involved in empire building. However, if you were to look at a world map and pinpoint American held territories, you would have to conclude the U.S. clearly qualifies as an empire building nation. Many of the countries acquired by the U.S. were essential for America to become a major world power in commerce and to protect its shores along the Atlantic Ocean, and Pacific Ocean. Other acquisitions were pursued to satisfy Americas' quest for expansionism as expressed by the doctrine of Manifest Destiny, where America would rule the North American continent from sea to sea. In the 1800s, to achieve expansionism and acquire vast territories, America went to war with England, Spain, and Mexico, including the mass pogrom of genocide and relocation of Native Americans.

By the 1900s, expansionism by means of war was no longer a viable option. The U.S. would have to find a new approach for empire building. The American policy of Protectorate Nation would be the new instrument for protecting American investments and economic development in Latin America. Under this concept, the U.S. would assume military control over a country with huge American investments in mining, sugar cane, oil, and other commercial interests. It would unilaterally declare that the affected nation was unable to govern itself, American lives were in danger, and American business interests would suffer losses. The U.S. would send a military force to occupy the country and remain there until it believed there was sufficient political and economic stability to remove its' army of occupation. In some cases the U.S. would impose a puppet government that was beholden to American interests. Taking control of a country to achieve American economic gains included Cuba in 1898, Colombia in 1904, to build the Panama Canal, Hawaii in 1893-1898, and the Philippines in 1898. Moreover, while the Mexican Revolution was in full force, President Wilson ordered that three Latin American countries be placed under Protectorate Nation status. Also, on June 19, 1916, under the Bryan-Chamorro Treaty, Nicaragua became a protectorate nation under U.S. control. The U.S. wanted to ensure that no other country would invade Nicaragua to build another "Panama Canal." On July 28, 1915, 330 U.S. Marines landed in Haiti to protect American investments in sugar cane. On May 15, 1916, the U.S. assumed full control of the Dominican Republic to protect its investments in sugar cane.

The initiative for the annexation of Mexico's five northern states had the support of leading American business interests, including John Hays Hammond, executive for the American Smelting and Refining Company, the largest operator of mines in the State of Chihuahua. It was also supported by Otto Khan, a financier, who was on record that Mexico's northern states should become independent, comparable to the action taken by the State of Texas. (William Walker also held that same belief when he invaded Baja California.)

Mexico in Danger of Protectorate Nation Status

If Villa had been taken prisoner by General Pershing, the stage would have been set for expansionist and yellow journalism to take charge of American policy. American business interests with huge land, cattle, and mining operations in Mexico's northern states had been supporters of expansionism for many years. One of the main supporters was Senator Albert Fall of New Mexico, who owned large tracts of land and silver mines in Chihuahua. He was already on record that the U.S. should take control of Mexico's northern states. William Randolph Hearst, the newspaper magnate who owned the Barbacoa Ranch with over one million acres of land in the State of Chihuahua, was another zealous supporter. Hearst believed that Mexico would offer very little resistance if the U.S. occupied Mexico's northern states. (Hearst and former Undersecretary of the U.S. Navy, Theodore Roosevelt, were the principal war mongers to occupy Cuba in 1898.)

Right after Villa attacked Columbus, newspapers all over the United States demanded retribution and intervention. On March 11, 1916, the San Francisco Examiner, a Hearst Newspaper, published the following headline:

> "Carranza sorry [that] Villa perpetrated Columbus massacre, but withholds consent to American pursuit of Villa and his Cutthroat Band of marauders, 3,000 strong ..."

On March 10, 1916, the New York Times wrote:

> "Following the news of the Villa raid, Senator Albert Fall of New Mexico announced that he had prepared a resolution authorizing the recruiting of 500,000 men to intervene in Mexico ..."

On March 10, 1916, the New York World wrote:

"Nothing less than Villa's life can atone for the outrage at Columbus, N. M. Whether or not, he led the raid in person, he unquestionably planned it, and the guerillas that executed it belonged to his forces. Every drop of American blood shed at Columbus is on his hands ..."

William Randolph Hearst and his 13 newspaper empire had a history of pursuing expansion. In 1898, six weeks before the war with Spain, the Hearst newspapers sent an emissary to Spain saying that the U.S. would declare war if Spain did not leave Cuba. On another occasion, when the Hearst correspondent, Fredrick Remington, operating out of Cuba informed Hearst that war was not likely with Spain, Hearst told the correspondent, "You furnish the pictures, and I will furnish the war."

History of Dominance over Mexico by the United States

In addition to the advocates for expansion and yellow journalism, Mexico was faced with historical record of the U.S. in taking land from Mexico. One example was the Texas Revolt of 1836, when General Santa Anna was held prisoner, until he agreed to cede Tejas to the Anglo-Texans. The agreement signed by General Santa Anna was never approved the Mexican Government, nonetheless, the U.S. assumed full occupation of Texas. In the war with Mexico of 1846, when Mexico was defeated by the U.S., Mexico had no choice but to acquiesce to demands of the U.S. Mexico was told that if it did not agree to cede the California, Arizona, and New Mexico Territories, then it would risk losing all of Mexico to the U.S.

By 1916, President Wilson would not have been able to overcome the pressure by American land barons and business interests, supported by yellow journalism, to punish Mexico. The expansionists would have overcome the objections of President Wilson by making it clear that the Mexican Government had proven incapable of protecting American lives and business interests. American financiers would have mobilized American newspapers and their political lobbyists would have converged on Congress to pressure President Wilson to place the five northern states under Protectorate Nation Status. (See map at end of chapter.)

Full occupation of Mexico was not a viable option in 1916, for the principal reason that the Monroe Doctrine had run its course and other nations would take issue with the U.S. for being imperialistic by occupying all of Mexico. A new scheme would have to be found. Such a scheme could be a negotiated settlement whereby the U.S. would assume control of the five Mexican states of Sonora, Chihuahua, Coahuila, Nuevo Leon, and Tamaulipas under the concept of Protectorate Nation. The arrangement could include the occupation of the mentioned states for a period of 20 years. At the end of 20 years, the populace could vote to remain Mexican or become part of the U.S. In the meantime, the U.S. would obligate itself to invest twenty million dollars each year to improve the infrastructure of each state, including a new Port of Entry from the Sea of Cortez, along the Arizona border. A seaport in Arizona would be beneficial for commercial development in the states of Arizona and New Mexico, since these states do not have seafaring capabilities

At the end of this chapter, the authors offer a Theoretical Protectorate Nation Agreement between the U.S. and Mexico. Presented is a map showing the Protectorate territories to be established by War Plan Green.

Failure to capture Pancho Villa

In 1916, the United States was poised to take more land from Mexico. With 10,000 American troops in the interior of Mexico and 140,000 additional troops deployed along the Mexican border, there was little Mexico could do to prevent such a takeover. The expansionist would argue that: we are here in Mexico, we have 10,000 American troops, we have Pancho Villa as a prisoner, and Carranza can't do anything about it.

In the final analysis, the people of Mexico may be deeply indebted to Pancho Villa because he managed to evade capture by General Pershing. Without capturing Pancho Villa, the U.S. had no calling card to make any demands on Mexico, regardless of how large an army was deployed and prepared to invade Mexico.

As mentioned, Pancho Villa was perhaps more guilty than other generals of the Revolution regarding atrocities and confiscation of property, but all civil wars are wrought with danger, death and destruction.[9] Moreover, one must keep in mind that Villa was being persecuted because Carranza wanted to ensure the Presidency for himself. This meant Villa was an obstacle that had to be removed by any means necessary, including defamation and subterfuge.

In ten years of revolutionary warfare, Pancho Villa proved he was the most astute and elusive guerilla warrior of the Revolution. He proved it to President Diaz, General Pascual Orozco, General Huerta, Primer Jefe Carranza, General Pershing, and President Wilson. With the exception of Pascual Orozco, each of them had an overwhelming military force and superior armaments, yet none of them were able to destroy Villa. Quite the

---

[9] For example, referring to modern warfare, at the end of WW II, in 1945, when the Russians captured Berlin, they were accused of having raped over 90,000 German women of all ages. In 1944, some members of the elite American Airborne had their testicles cut off by embittered German troops when they parachuted on the Normandy beaches.

contrary, instead of destroying Villa, he was granted amnesty and given a hacienda in 1920 to retire from the Revolution, an action for which the U.S. did not offer any resistance.

Theoretical Military Orders Issued to General Pershing

[The following theoretical military orders refer to the author's analysis and inferences of potential military orders that could have been given to General Pershing]

Military Order 1916-4-16

To: General John Pershing, American Punitive Expedition

From: General Frederick Funston, Commander Southwest Border Region

The following war plans apply to all military personnel involved in prosecuting military operations in Mexico.

(1) United States Naval and Army forces are to occupy Mexico for the purpose of finding a military resolution regarding the inability of de facto President Venustiano Carranza to control the forces of General Villa along the United States and Mexican International Border.

(2) Naval forces shall execute a Naval Blockade at the Port of Veracruz, and await further instructions for the occupation of Mexico City by United States Marines. Land forces under General Pershing are to occupy Parral, Chihuahua to ensure rapid movement via the railroad axis of Torreon-Zacatecas-Mexico City.

(3) When captured, General Villa shall be held as a prisoner of war. His release will be contingent upon a diplomatic settlement with the government of General Venustiano Carranza regarding United States financial and economic interests along the Mexican Border States, of Sonora, Chihuahua, Coahuila, Nuevo Leon, and Tamaulipas.

(4) Once full military occupation of Mexico City has been vested, United States Diplomats will arrive to negotiate with the government of Carranza for cash purchase the aforementioned states, or to consider placing of the

aforementioned states as a Protectorate of the United States.

(5) Prior governmental experience emanating from the Treaty of Guadalupe of 1848, Annexation of Texas, 1836, and the Gadsden Purchase shall serve to guide negotiations.

Protectorate Nation Agreement

[The following theoretical Protectorate Nation Accord refers to the author's analysis and inferences in the event the U.S. occupied the five northern states of Mexico]

ACCORD and PROTECTORATE NATION AGREEMENT between the UNITED STATES of AMERICA and the REPUBLIC of MEXICO

Whereas, it is desirous for The Republic of Mexico and The United States of America to remain in a state of peace and thereby provide for each other a mutually satisfactory understanding regarding civility and economic freedom, and

Whereas, it is a necessity for both nations to maintain law and order along the contiguous border states that abound both nations, and

Whereas, it is in the highest interest of both nations to do the utmost in their power to protect the civilian population and the economic interests of the citizens of both nations,

Therefore, acting in the best interest of the common good, both nations hereby agree to the following provisions:

Article I.   The Republic of Mexico hereby places the states of Sonora, Chihuahua, Coahuila, Nuevo Leon, and Tamaulipas under the protectorate of the United States for a period of twenty years, after which time a plebiscite shall be conducted to determine a proper form of government.

Article II.   The populace and citizenry of the aforementioned states shall enjoy the full measure of Republic of Mexico citizenship, including, but not limited to ownership and transfer of land, voting rights, ability to hold elected office, conduct business, and public education.

Article III.   In the interest of the free flow of commerce and mutual development of economic resources, the United States unequivocally and without reservation agrees that the aforementioned states shall be entitled to speak and conduct business in a language of their choice and that all laws, court mandates, administrative procedures and local governance shall be printed in the Spanish and English languages.

Article IV. The United States of America for a period of twenty years shall invest $20,000,000 annually in each of the aforementioned states for the development of infrastructure or enhancement of roads, bridges, canals, port of entry construction, and a national railway system, and the development of Port of Entry from the Sea of Cortes in Baja California to the State of Arizona in the United States.

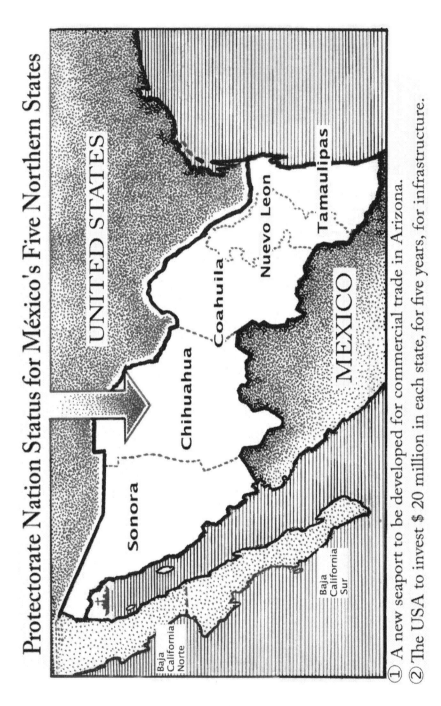

Protectorate Nation Status for México's Five Northern States

① A new seaport to be developed for commercial trade in Arizona.
② The USA to invest $ 20 million in each state, for five years, for infrastructure.

Article V.   The United States shall establish a Border Resolution Commission to properly compensate the citizens of Mexico for any loss of life; or destruction of property arising from the expeditionary force conducted by the United States under the command of General John Pershing.

Article VI.   To ensure the domestic tranquility of the Republic of Mexico, by declaration of this document, the United States of America hereby duly informs all foreign powers and nations that the United States of America shall provide any and all economic or military assistance to The Republic of Mexico, if and when requested to do so.

Ratification.   This instrument of agreement for an ACCORD AND PROTECTORATE STATUS between the two nations shall be legally recognized and thereafter executed upon the approval by two thirds vote by the Congress of the United States and the Congress of The Republic of Mexico. The Agreement shall be considered fully executed when signed by the representatives for each respective country.

Duly Executed ACCORD AND PROTECTORATE NATION STATUS
City of Saltillo, State of Coahuila, Republic of Mexico
For the Republic of Mexico: Gen. Alvaro Obregón, Special Emissary.
For the United States of America: Gen. John H. Pershing, Special Emissary
General Alvaro Obregón /signed/
General John Pershing /signed/

Part Four – Into the Sunset

Chapter XIV. Amnesty for Pancho Villa

By 1919, Pancho Villa was the last major figure of the Revolution to be fighting against the Carranza regime. Carranza had consolidated his power base in Mexico City; in 1917, he had been elected President of Mexico and in 1919, he had eliminated Emiliano Zapata by orchestrating his assassination at the Hacienda Chinemeca. While Carranza was gaining power, Villa had suffered a number of major setbacks, he had lost his chief generals, Tomas Urbina, Rodolfo Fierro, and General Felipe Ángeles, Villa's most influential general, had gone to live in the U.S.

Since Villa's fortunes were on the decline, Carranza believed the time was right to destroy Villa's Army, and bring the Revolution to a final conclusion. Carranza assembled a powerful army under the command of General Joaquin Amaro and ordered him to destroy Villa at his home base in the State of Chihuahua.

When Villa learned that General Amaro was on his way to Chihuahua, as he had done so often when the odds were against him, he decided to attack Ciudad Juarez, Chihuahua, to show Carranza that he was still a formidable opponent. Besides being of strategic military value, Ciudad Juarez was an important city with an ample supply of horses, munitions, and provisions. Villa decided to attack June 15, 1919, but on the day of the attack, he fell ill, and assigned the task of taking Ciudad Juarez to General Martin Lopez. The city was quickly taken by surprise and the Villistas forced the Federales to retreat to nearby Fort Hidalgo.

The Villistas, having been deprived of city life after so many months of guerilla warfare, let their guard down and began to drink and plunder the city. While the Villistas were enjoying the benefits of their victory, two Carranza officers at Fort Hidalgo entered into an argument when one officer accused the other of cowardice for having left behind the Mexican flag during their retreat.

The accused officer reacted by returning to the city with a determined force to retrieve the flag. When he arrived, he found the city was not properly defended by the Villistas, and the Carranza troops were able to retake the city. Villa now decided to take personal charge of a second attack. Within hours, Villa had retaken the city and was about to destroy the remaining Carranza troops at Fort Hidalgo, when the U.S. Cavalry arrived to confront the Villistas. General James B. Erwin, Commander of U.S. forces in El Paso, with 1,000 American troops ordered a cavalry attack on the Villistas because a few American citizens and two American soldiers had been wounded by stray bullets. Villa was not able to engage the well-equipped American Cavalry and was forced to make an immediate retreat. By this time, the American Cavalry had standing orders to immediately retaliate against any intrusion or damage to American lives or property along the border. The ability to pursue across the border was the outcome of the "Hot Pursuit" policy agreed to between the U.S. and the Carranza government in 1916, when Villa had raided Columbus, New Mexico.

After leaving Ciudad Juarez, Villa decided to attack the City of Durango, in the State of Durango. To make sure his rear was covered during the attack, he ordered officers Ricardo Michel and José Galviz to tear up the railroad tracks leading from Torreon, Coahuila, to the City of Durango, but the officers did not follow through on his orders. As he started the attack, from the horizon, Villa could see Federal troops approaching by train, and once again he was forced to make a hasty departure. During the retreat from City of Durango, Villa lost General Martin Lopez, one of his most trusted soldiers who had been with him since the start of the Revolution.

Villa now began to think he should leave Chihuahua and operate in the State of Coahuila. Villa reasoned that he was losing the support of the people of Chihuahua, and his army was beginning to dwindle due to casualties and desertion among the ranks. As he moved from village to village, he found it necessary to take hostages. He wanted to be sure the people in the villages he left behind would not turn against him. As he entered each new village, he would release the previous hostages and take on new hostages.

After his retreat from the City of Durango, Villa started to think seriously about retiring from the Revolution. In the previous three years he had suffered several major setbacks: the pursuit by General Pershing; the loss of generals General Rodolfo Fierro, who died in quicksand in Chihuahua, and Tomas Urbina, whom he shot for deserting him in the battle for the City of Celaya; the loss of General Felipe Ángeles; and the recent loss of General Martin Lopez. Also to be considered was the loss of his fellow patriot Emiliano Zapata, the strong man in the South, who had been assassinated only two months earlier by orders of Carranza.

Just when Villa believed he was running out of options to survive the Revolution, the political landscape began to change in Mexico City. According the Constitution of Mexico, Carranza could not run for reelection for the presidency of 1920. However, since Carranza still craved to be at the center of power, he declared he would support Ignacio Bonilla to be the next

President of Mexico. Carranza's support for Ignacio Bonilla upset General Alvaro Obregón, who had already declared he wanted to be elected president in 1920. After having won so many battles for Carranza, and being his loyal supporter throughout the Revolution, Obregón believed he had earned the support of Carranza for the presidency. Moreover, Ignacio Bonilla had not been involved in any of the military campaigns of the Revolution, he was not well known throughout the country, and many believed that Bonilla would fall under the control of Carranza. In addition, by 1920, Carranza's Presidency had begun to fall apart. He was accused of abusing his administration: he had enriched his pockets by accumulating land and money, several of his generals had become millionaires through graft and selling protection to the Hacendados, and now he was in open conflict with General Obregón. The rupture between Carranza and Obregón became public on April 20, 1920, when a revolt led by supporters of Obregón declared Carranza was no longer President and voted for Adolfo de la Huerta, Governor of Sonora, to serve as Provisional President to finish Carranza's presidential term.

When hostilities opened up between Carranza and Obregón, representatives of the Obregón faction from the State of Sonora offered to reconcile with Villa, if Villa would side with the Obregón people. Based on the offer by the Obregón faction, and since Carranza and Obregón were involved in open conflict, Villa got the idea that perhaps he could negotiate peaceful terms with Provisional President Adolfo de la Huerta, and retire from the Revolution. Villa had also considered aligning himself with the Obregón faction, but unfortunately, Villa was not able to explore reconciliation because the conflict between Carranza and Obregón ended in a matter of days when Carranza was assassinated in May 1920. Carranza knew the nation had turned against him and he decided to leave Mexico. His plan to escape was to commandeer a military train with 300 soldiers, and over $136,000,000 in silver and gold (including the machines to make coins) from the Mexican treasury and leave Mexico City for the Port of Veracruz. His train was intercepted near Veracruz, where he was betrayed and assassinated on May 21, 1920.

Although the offer by Obregón supporters quickly ended because Carranza had been assassinated, Villa now decided to approach General Plutarco Calles, whom he had fought against at Agua Prieta, Sonora. Villa suggested to General Calles that he could retire from the Revolution if he were given a hacienda to farm and made the commander of the Rurales in Chihuahua. General Calles rejected the offer; instead he suggested that Villa resettle in the State of Sonora, his home state. But Villa did not want to settle in Sonora; he wanted to stay in Chihuahua. Most likely, Villa believed that if settled in Sonora, General Calles's home state, he could be easily disposed of by General Calles. Villa was not familiar with the terrain in Sonora; moreover he knew he would not have the support of the villagers of Sonora, as he had in Chihuahua.

Villa next contacted General Ignacio Enriquez, who was in charge of the strongest military force in the State of Chihuahua. It is not clear why Villa contacted General Enriquez for a peace settlement. Villa knew that General Enriquez could not be trusted because they had been bitter enemies during all the years of the Revolution. Since Villa did not trust Enriquez, he decided to plan a trap to find out if Enriquez was going to betray him. Once a location was agreed to for a meeting of the two generals, Villa setup a phony campsite to make it look as if it was occupied by the Villistas. When the troops of General Enriquez arrived in the evening, they rushed into the campsite firing their weapons hoping to kill Pancho Villa, but the Villistas had hidden outside the campsite and were able to destroy the troops sent by General Enriquez.

After the betrayal by General Enriquez, Villa decided it would be wiser to make direct contact with Provisional President De la Huerta. When Villa contacted De la Huerta, he was surprised to learn that De la Huerta was more than willing to come to a peace settlement. De la Huerta immediately arranged for Elias Torres, a newspaperman and his confidant, to meet with Villa in Chihuahua to discuss the terms of a settlement. Villa and his representatives met with Elias Torres at the Hacienda Encinillas on July 2, 1920. Villa proposed that he be granted the following: a hacienda for himself and the soldiers, widows and orphans of his Division del Norte; authorization to command 500 soldiers to stop the violence and thievery in Chihuahua; and De la Huerta to conduct free elections in the State of Chihuahua. If De la Huerta were to agree to these terms, Villa pledged to be loyal to whoever became president of Mexico in 1920 election (quite possibly General Obregón). Further, he would call for a truce with all his enemies and would not seek retribution against his enemies. To ensure that the terms of the agreement would be complied with, Villa requested that generals Benjamin Hill, Plutarco Calles, and Alvaro Obregón sign the peace agreement.

The agreement with De la Huerta almost fell apart when Elias Torres allowed the agreement to be published in the newspapers. Upon hearing that Villa was going to receive amnesty, General Obregón notified De la Huerta that he was unequivocally opposed to the agreement. General Obregón believed that Villa should not be forgiven for several reasons: damage to property; confiscation of haciendas; and the atrocities committed by Villa. General Obregón also believed that the U.S. might take a hard line and oppose amnesty for Villa because the U.S. was still upset about the raid by Villa on Columbus, New Mexico, as well as the embarrassment and the failure of General Pershing to capture Pancho Villa. Quite reasonably, General Obregon believed that the U.S. might possibly try to intervene against Mexico to seek justice for the damages and loss of life at Columbus.

The inflexible position taken by General Obregón forced De la Huerta to suspend the negotiations. He notified the press that Elias Torres spoke prematurely and that he was not acting in an official capacity. Villa could see that securing an agreement for peace would require a new strategy. He decided to conduct his military operations in the rich agricultural State of Coahuila. During the years of the Revolution, the State of Coahuila had not been as heavily ravaged as the State of Chihuahua. Villa believed that if he brought the Revolution to the State of Coahuila, his military activities would certainly attract the attention of Provisional President De la Huerta. Villa also believed De la Huerta would be alarmed by taking the Revolution to a new territory, especially in Carranza's own home state of Coahuila along the U.S. border. In addition, by moving his operations to the city of Sabinas, Villa would be less than one hundred miles from the U.S. border, at Eagle Pass, Texas, and once again he could raise the specter of U.S. intervention, something that Provisional President De la Huerta would not welcome. To reach Coahuila, Villa pushed his soldiers across seven hundred miles of desert between the states of Chihuahua and Coahuila, a tract of desert known as the "Boslon de Mapimi." By the time Villa reached Sabinas, Coahuila, he had lost many men due to thirst and starvation. When Villa reached Coahuila, everyone was impressed that he had accomplished an impossible feat, and in the process he proved that he was still a great guerilla fighter.

After reaching Sabinas, Villa contacted De la Huerta to restart a peace agreement. Villa had the concurrence of both General Benjamin Hill and General Plutarco Calles, but General Obregón continued to refuse to sign the agreement and once again Obregón made it clear to De la Huerta that he did not believe that Villa was entitled to forgiveness and compensation. With the signatures of De la Huerta, and Generals Hill and Calles in hand, Villa decided to sign the agreement. He reasoned he had the main signatory to the agreement, Provisional President De la Huerta, the ultimate authority in Mexico.

Eventually, two months later, General Obregón sent a message to De la Huerta that he would not stand in the way of the agreement. Perhaps General Obregón hoped that since he was going to be elected President in 1920, he did not want the country to accuse him of being against ending the Revolution. Also, if Villa started military operations in the State of Coahuila, the people would blame General Obregón for obstructing peace, and prolonging the Revolution, and possibly initiate another intervention by the U.S.

The final peace agreement was signed June 26, 1920, in Sabinas, Coahuila. The terms of the agreement included:

- Villa was granted the Hacienda El Canutillo, a 25,000 acre ranch in the State of Durango

- Some eight hundred (800) of his men were allowed to join the Federal Army and retain their military rank.

- Some 200 Villistas were allowed to retire to live with Pancho Villa at El Canutillo.

- Villa was granted fifty (50) Villistas as his personal escort, at government expense.

- Villa was granted amnesty for all past violations or indiscretions.

- Villa agreed to retire to private life and not participate in any insurrections against the government.

When Villa arrived at El Canutillo, he found the hacienda was in shambles. He quickly rallied his men to recondition the hacienda, start buying livestock and plant crops. He introduced modern farming practices when he bought three tractors for plowing and cultivating the land. The hacienda became a colony for 200 Villistas. They opened shops in carpentry, electrical and equipment repair, welding, saddlery and blacksmithing, and also added a mill for grinding corn. Villa also fulfilled a lifelong dream by opening a school for three hundred children of the Revolution. He named the school the "General Felipe Ángeles School" in honor of his beloved general who taught him about education, military tactics, and decent treatment of prisoners.

Villa's first wife, Luz Corral, and their children came to live at El Canutillo, but soon Villa, the eternal womanizer, brought his paramour, Austreberta Renteria to live at the hacienda as well. Villa used the ruse that he wanted Luz, who was an expert seamstress, to show Austreberta how to make clothing. This, of course, caused friction between the women, and Luz Corral left to live in the home that Villa and Luz had constructed in Chihuahua City. Villa, who was known to love children, was able to bring many of his children born out of wedlock to live with him at El Canutillo. Needless to say, the time Villa spent at El Canutillo was the happiest time of his life. He was assassinated on June 20, 1923, when he went to Parral, Chihuahua, to attend to business. Had he lived longer, Villa had planned to build a modern mill to process wheat, introduce a modern irrigation system, and build a railroad to Parral. With the success Villa had with his ranching operations, it is doubtful he would again be involved in any military campaign. However, on the other hand, he might be involved in endorsing political issues or certain candidates for office.

Chapter XV.   Assassination of Pancho Villa

Pancho Villa was assassinated on July 20, 1923, in Parral, Chihuahua, a small mining town of 25,000 inhabitants. This was not the first time an attempt was made on his life. Earlier, on July 10, Villa had stayed at the Hotel Hidalgo, which he owned with his third wife, Manuela Casas. When he left the hotel that July morning to return to his ranch, a number of assassins were lying in wait to shoot him as he departed Parral. The assassins were not able to execute Villa because at the last moment a group of school children marching to school blocked their line of fire.

On July 19, Villa had visited Parral to take care of business related to his farming operations. When he left on the morning of July 20 to return to his ranch, he was driving a 1920 Dodge open air car accompanied by six of his beloved Dorados. To leave Parral, he would have to pass through the intersection of Benito Juarez and Gabino Barreda streets. He would then come to a complete stop at Gabino Barreda and then make a right turn. As the car neared the intersection, it slowed down almost to a full stop. At that moment, by a prearranged signal, one of the conspirators raised his arms and shouted *Viva Villa*, an emotional expression that Villa had heard many times from his supporters. But this time he could not conceive that the *Viva Villa* shout was the signal for eight men who were hidden in a two story building to open fire. Villa's car was hit with 40 dum-dum rifle bullets (bullets that have a blunted tip to cause internal damage). Villa, who was driving the car, died instantly when he was hit with eight bullets. Manuel Trillo and Daniel Tamayo, his regular driver, were also killed instantly. Ramon Contreras and Claro

Hurtado escaped to a nearby bridge. Hurtado was fatally shot, but Contreras was able to kill one of the assassins. Ramon Contreras was the only Villista to escape the ambush.

Villa knew his life was in constant danger and whenever he visited Parral, he was accompanied by a dozen or more of his cavalry escort. He made an exception on his last trip because he wanted to visit Parral and return as soon as possible to his ranch. He believed that a cavalry escort would only serve to slow him down, so he decided to travel by automobile, at a faster pace.

There are many reasons why Villa was assassinated. Perhaps one of his enemies wanted revenge because Villa had confiscated their property and they had lost all their wealth, or he had executed a family member, or maybe a general Villa had defeated wanted revenge.

It is difficult to determine with certainty who was responsible for the assassination of Villa. Two prominent names linked to the assassination are General Alvaro Obregón, who was the President of Mexico at the time, and Plutarco Calles, Minister of Defense in charge of the Army; both were longtime adversaries of Villa. In addition, Colonel Felix Lara, the Federal officer in charge of the Parral garrison, was not at Parral at the time of the assassination. For some mysterious reason, Colonel Lara had left for a nearby town to practice for a parade, and when he returned he made no effort to pursue the assassins. His claim that he had no horses for the pursuit was a rather suspicious claim.

Although many plots and subplots were advanced regarding the person or persons responsible, no investigation has provided conclusive proof regarding the circumstances and the motives for the assassination. Jesus Salas Barraza, a minor legislator with the State of Durango, confessed to the crime. He was sentenced to prison for twenty years by the State of Chihuahua. However, after two months in prison, he was pardoned by Ignacio Enriquez, the Governor of Chihuahua, and a die-hard adversary of Villa. Months later, Barraza was allowed to join the Federal Army to fight against de la Huerta, a presidential candidate opposing General Obregón. It was also speculated that Meliton Lozoya was one of the assassins. Lozoya had been the administrator for the Hacienda Canutillo prior to the time Villa was granted amnesty. When Villa found out that Lozoya had removed personal property before he assumed ownership, Villa went after him. He told Lozoya that he was to return the stolen property or pay its value, and if not, Villa would kill him.

The only known fact about the assassination is that someone wanted Villa dead, and unless it is known who the true assassin was, the world will never know the real reason for the assassination. After all allegations, plots, and subplots are examined, a number of fingers point to Alvaro Obregón, for the following reasons:

- Considering the logistics involved in organizing and executing a plan against such a high profile target, the plan had to be sanctioned by a person with a very high level of authority. Such an authority would have to have the ability to organize the various elements of the plan, and provide protection for the conspirators in the event they got caught. In addition, the crime would not be committed unless the perpetrator was offered protection and some type of compensation.

- The main conspirator would have to have deep rooted reasons for the removal of Villa. General Obregón is the main person with ample reasons to assassinate Villa.

From 1914 to 1920, Villa and General Obregón were arch enemies. In the two battles for the City of Celaya in 1915, Villa mounted two vicious attacks that cost General Obregón many causalities, and he was almost defeated. In addition, in a subsequent battle for Leon, Guanajuato, General Obregón lost an arm when he came under attack by Villa's artillery. In 1913, in the campaign to remove Huerta, Carranza sent General Obregón as an emissary to visit Villa in an attempt to reconcile the differences between Villa and Carranza. However, unknown to General Obregón, Carranza had also sent a small unit to assassinate Villa. When Villa found out about the assassination plot, he blamed General Obregón and had him arrested. Villa had every intention of placing General Obregón before a firing squad, but the general was able to convince Villa that he was not part of the plot to assassinate him.

- When Villa was assassinated, General Obregón, who was then the President of Mexico, was asked to conduct an investigation regarding the assassination. Since Salas Barraza had confessed to the crime, General Obregón only conducted a half-halfhearted investigation. Salas Barraza was sentenced to twenty years in prison but was later pardoned by General Enriquez, the Governor of Chihuahua and an ally of General Obregón, an action that appears to have been sanctioned by Obregón as the President of Mexico. Additionally, after Salas Barraza was pardoned, he joined the Federal Army as a Colonel, an action that raises suspicions regarding the complicity of General Obregón. After Salas Barraza was pardoned, he made a request to interview Obregón, a request that was granted. It seems highly irregular that the President of Mexico would grant an interview to a convicted criminal who had assassinated a citizen under the protection (amnesty for Pancho Villa) of his Presidency.

- General Martinez, Commander for Chihuahua, and Colonel Felix Lara, in charge of the Parral garrison, were never investigated to determine why they themselves did not take aggressive action to capture the assailants or to determine if they had been co-conspirators. No investigation was conducted as to why Colonel Lara was not able to find horses to pursue the assailants or why the telephone lines were down for six hours. On the other hand, if the Villistas at El Canutillo ranch had been immediately informed about the assassination, they most certainly would have relentlessly pursued the assailants until they were captured.

- Another reason that points to General Obregón is the fact that he was upset over the amnesty given to Pancho Villa in 1920 by Provisional President de la Huerta. General Obregón was adamant that Villa was not entitled to amnesty, and in particular he was dissatisfied with the generous terms awarded to Villa. When Villa agreed to terms for an amnesty, he requested that General Benjamin Hill, Plutarco Calles, and Alvaro Obregón sign the agreement, but General Obregón refused to sign. Villa obviously wanted assurances other than the signature of Provisional President Adlofo de la Huerta that his amnesty would not be rescinded, in case

217

Obregón was elected President of Mexico.

In the final analysis, Obregón was suspected of ordering the assassination of Villa because he had engaged Villa in several bloody battles, had once been his prisoner, and was once almost executed by Villa, In addition, he did not conduct an aggressive investigation, and he appeared to have sanctioned the conduct of Salas Barraza. Also, it appears that Obregón sanctioned the pardon granted to Barraza by Governor Enriquez, and later permitted Salas Barraza to enlist in the army as Colonel, in an army under his command.

Perhaps General Obregón wanted Villa out of the way because he believed that Villa was a threat to his Presidency. Many reporters and dignitaries visited Villa at his hacienda and constantly asked him if he would return to the Revolution. Also there were some intelligence reports that Villa had a large cache of arms hidden at the Hacienda El Canutillo in preparation for another revolt. It is reasonable to assume that General Obregón could not tolerate another revolt if he expected to be recognized by the new U.S. President Warren Harding.

Villa was buried on July 21, the day following his assassination, in the cemetery of Parral. He was placed in a carriage and led by two black horses to the cemetery. None of the Villistas, or his Dorados was able to attend the burial because they were guarding El Canutillo from federal troops who had arrived and threatened to occupy the ranch. Also, Villa's body was not allowed to be buried in the mausoleum that he had constructed in Chihuahua City, because Governor Enriquez, his staunch enemy, had decreed that the ownership documents for the burial site were not in proper order.

On February 6, 1926, the caretaker of the cemetery at Parral reported that Villa's grave had been violated and his head had been removed. Emil Holmdahl and Albert Corral were investigated, but no evidence was found to file criminal charges. Speculation was rampant as to why Villa's head was stolen. One allegation is that General Obregón wanted Villa's head as a trophy; or General Arnulfo Gomez wanted to have Villa's head examined to determine his military genius; or the head was sold to the Skulls and Bones Society, an organization affiliated with Yale University. Two scenarios are possible as to why Villa's decapitated head was never found: the person(s) who stole Villa's head probably botched the job if they didn't have the proper chemicals to preserve the head, and thus Villa's head was rendered useless; or once haven stolen the head, they realized they would be tracked with a vengeance by the Villistas, so they just decided to dispose of it leaving no trace as to its whereabouts.

Unfortunately, the world will never know.

Years after the Revolution ended, intellectuals, historians, and politicians continued to acknowledge the impact the revolutionaries made on the nation. To commemorate their contributions, the Mexican Government erected a National Monument to the Revolution in Mexico City. In November 1976, the body of Pancho Villa was removed from Parral and entombed in the National Monument, to accompany his beloved Francisco Madero.

Chapter XVI. The Downfall of Carranza

By 1920, Carranza had come to the end of his control of Mexico. The nation was well aware of the many incidents where he had failed to demonstrate statesmanship, and instead, had demonstrated vindictiveness towards his enemies. His indiscretions included corruption in his presidency, an ill-advised attempt to impose Ignacio Bonillas as President of Mexico, discord with General Alvaro Obregón, his effort to sabotage the Convention of Aguascalientes, his overt attempt to keep Pancho Villa from being the first general to enter Mexico City in the campaign against General Huerta, his punitive orders to assassinate Emiliano Zapata, and the malicious court martial that resulted in the execution of General Felipe Ángeles.

In the years that Carranza served as the Primer Jefe and later as President of Mexico, he made minimal effort to reconcile his differences with Villa and Zapata. While serving as Primer Jefe, Carranza could have established an International Commission of Latin American countries to settle his difference with the revolutionary forces of Villa and Zapata. He could have called upon the neighboring Latin American countries to establish a Commission to bring peace in Mexico. The Commission could have rendered a valuable service to resolve the issues of the Revolution and end the bloodshed and destruction of property. It is quite possible that Carranza did not want such a Commission because it would recommend that he remove himself as the Primer Jefe in order to restore stability in the nation, and this was something he was not willing to do. This was the case at the Convention of Aguascalientes of 1914 when he was asked to resign as Primer Jefe and allow Eulalio Gutierrez to serve as Provisional President until new elections could be held. Perhaps Carranza anticipated that if such a Commission had been established, it would ask him to resign and he wasn't about to give up the power he had claimed when he declared himself Primer Jefe, a power that had been sanctioned by President Wilson. From a careful review of the key turning points of the Revolution, one could reasonably conclude that Carranza coveted the Presidency as soon as President Madero was assassinated in 1913. And no one was going to interfere with his ambition for the Presidency because his ultimate ambition to become President was more important than reconciliation with Villa, Zapata, or Obregón.

At the Convention of Aguascalientes, Carranza could have brought an end to the Revolution if he had abided by the recommendation from the Convention for him to resign as Primer Jefe. The purpose of the Convention had been agreed to months earlier by the generals of the Revolution when it was planned that as soon as Huerta was removed, they would meet to elect a Provisional President. In accordance with the process approved, Eulalio Gutierrez was elected Provisional President until formal elections could be held. Carranza rejected the request by the Convention for him to resign. Once again, Carranza was afforded an opportunity to exercise statesmanship, but instead he chose to hold on to his power base. It is also important to note that when Carranza convened the Plan de Guadalupe in his home state of Coahuila, no one with a higher military rank than Colonel signed the Plan, including any of the major leaders of the Revolution, such as Villa, Zapata, or Obregón. Obviously, at that point in time, the leaders of the Revolution were more concerned with removing Huerta for his betrayal of President Madero, and little attention was paid to the fine print of the Plan de Guadalupe.

While in power, Carranza prepared a list of Hacendados Intervenidos (a select group of large land owners) who had supported General Huerta. He systematically charged them extra taxes and imposed monetary payments in retribution for supporting General Huerta. In the process, his favorite generals, who were responsible for collecting payments from the Hacendados Intervenidos, became millionaires, while many of the Hacendados affected by higher taxes went broke. In addition to collecting taxes, the generals offered protection against roaming bandit groups. The Madero family, one of the wealthiest families in Mexico, also went broke when they were included in Carranza's vendetta for retribution.

In 1919, Carranza made a determined effort to eliminate Emiliano Zapata, the bigger-than-life general from the South. General Zapata was assassinated on April 7, 1919, in an ambush set up by Colonel Refugio Guajardo under the authority of Carranza. General Ángeles was also eliminated when he was captured in the State of Chihuahua. Ángeles had left Mexico but returned to spend time with Villa to try to convince him to end the Revolution. Unable to convince General Villa, Ángeles decided to return to the U.S. On the way to the U.S., he was captured and taken to Chihuahua City for a court martial. Many influential people pleaded for General Ángeles to be sent to prison, but Carranza instructed that he be executed instead. The execution of Zapata and Ángeles was not necessary for Carranza to stay in power. His conduct in executing Ángeles is another example of his relentless quest to stay in power.

In the Presidential elections of 1920, Carranza decided not to support General Obregón for the Presidency. According to the Mexican Constitution, Carranza could not run for another term in

1920. To stay in power, he chose to support Ignacio Bonillas, an unknown candidate whom he could control. When it was clear that Obregón might win the election, Carranza attempted to have him arrested, but Obregón escaped to the State of Guerrero for protection.

All of these negative events eventually led to Carranza's downfall. Knowing that the nation was about to turn against him, he loaded a train with gold and silver bars and coins and had his soldiers take him to the Port of Veracruz to escape from Mexico. He was intercepted in the State of Puebla where he was assassinated by one of the generals supporting Obregón for the Presidency. It is ironic that Carranza died in the same manner that he had treated his adversaries, by assassination. After the demise of Carranza, General Obregón became the President of Mexico, but General Obregón was soon faced with the War of the Cristeros, a revolt promoted by the Catholic hierarchy.

Chapter XVII. The Myths of Pancho Villa

Many stories have been created about Pancho Villa, some are true, some are somewhat true, and others are pure fantasy. If you were to believe all these rumors, you would have to conclude the following: (1) Pancho Villa had at least one hundred wives; (2) he crossed the American border to attack the U.S. at least a dozen times; (3) he had hoards of gold hidden in the U.S. and in Mexico; and (4) he was the only general to conduct wholesale execution of captured prisoners.

The Many Wives of Pancho Villa

Villa was imbued with chicanery regarding women. He professed to have a great deal of respect for women, but in reality he considered them as compensation for being a leader of the

Revolution. As the elite general of the Division del Norte he was adored by many women, especially after gaining victories over the Federal troops in major battles, such as in Torreon, Chihuahua, Ciudad Juarez, and Zacatecas. He only had one legal wife, Luz Corral, whom he met in the small town of San Andres in 1911, during the first part of the Revolution. Luz and her mother operated a small dress shop when they were visited by Villa who wanted a custom shirt made. After a short courtship, they were married in her hometown in 1912. After the defeat of President Diaz in 1913, Luz and Pancho Villa, settled in Chihuahua City, where Villa bought Luz a home, and he went into business by opening three butcher shops. In the following years, Villa expanded the original home to become a large estate which they called Quinto Sol.

Throughout their marriage, Luz stayed in Chihuahua and did not accompany Villa on military campaigns. Villa did not want the distraction of a woman while planning and executing military engagements. (He also applied this principle to his beloved Dorados, by prohibiting them from having their women accompany them into battle; while on the other hand, he permitted the Soldaderas to accompany their loved ones into battle.)

In addition to Luz, Villa "married" several women in his lifetime. In some instances when Villa courted a woman, he would ask her if she wanted to get married. If she said yes, he would send for the appropriate local official to perform a sham marriage ceremony where no documents were signed or legally recorded. Villa believed that if a woman wished to be married, he should do so to protect her honor, without any intent of fulfilling any marriage vows. In later years, several women claimed they had a son or daughter out of wedlock with Villa, and since he loved children, in many cases, he accepted the children as his own and would provide for their education. By 1920, when he had received amnesty and a 25,000 acre ranch from the Government, he had many of the children come and live with him at his hacienda, El Canutillo, near the City of Parral.

When Villa died, he did not have a last will and testament designating his heirs and beneficiaries. This caused legal problems for many years because there was no one person designated to administer his estate. By the time of his death, Villa was well to do. In addition to the hacienda, he owned several homes in Chihuahua, as well as a home and the Hotel Hidalgo in the City of Parral. In addition, he may have hoarded money, silver, or gold, on his ranch. Four women claimed to have legal rights to his estate: Luz Corral whom he legally married in 1912 (who gave him a daughter who died at an early age); Austerberta Renteria, his mistress at El Canutillo ranch (who bore him two sons, Hipolito and Francisco); Manuela Casas, who administered the Hotel Hidalgo in Parral (one son); and Soledad Seanez, who lived nearby in Parral (no children). After several years of litigation and appeal by the several wives to the Government of Mexico regarding property ownership, President Alvaro Obregón eventually declared that Luz Corral was the only true widow. President Obregón reasoned that Villa was legally married to Luz since he had not obtained a legal divorce to marry the other women. Luz Villa never remarried and throughout her lifetime she held onto strong memories of her life with Pancho Villa. She converted the Quinto Sol estate, in Chihuahua City, into a museum of the Revolution where she displayed many of Villa's possessions and the Dodge car involved in his assassination. Several years later, Luz wrote a book about her life with her husband, "Pancho Villa en la intimidad."

Allegation of Atrocities

The available evidence supports the notion that Villa committed more atrocities than any other leader of the Revolution. There are several things to keep in mind regarding Villa's conduct. First, except for General Felipe Ángeles who did not execute a prisoner, all the generals executed prisoners by firing squad or by hanging. Second, Villa was brought into the Revolution because of his expertise in guerilla warfare and his tactics in punishing the enemy. When Francisco Madero and Abraham Gonzalez recruited Villa to join the Revolution, they were aware that Villa would fight with a "take the gloves off" attitude. After all, he had been a cattle rustler and bandit in the hills of Chihuahua and Durango for sixteen years. Third, the execution of prisoners during the Revolution was ordered by Primer Jefe Venustiano Carranza, who based his decree on the war of Reform. Fourth, Villa became more vicious about executing prisoners in 1915, after he lost the Battle for the City of Agua Prieta, when he learned that President Wilson had authorized the transporting of the Mexican Army from Eagle Pass, Texas, to Douglas, Arizona, to destroy Villa.

During the Pershing Expedition, Villa was accused of cutting off the ears of his enemies. This was not a widespread practice, but it did occur, when one of Villa's officers, Baudelio Uribe, captured a prisoner who had served with Carranza's Army. The prisoner was set free, but his ear was cutoff as a reminder that if he was caught fighting against Villa again, he would be executed.

The atrocities committed by all of the Revolutionaries are not excusable, but one must remember that the Revolution was a "death to the end" struggle by adversaries bent on destroying each other. In addition, the Revolutionaries did not have the capability to hold prisoners. Also, they feared that if prisoners were set free, they would quite likely return to their respective

227

unit to continue fighting in the Revolution. The only exception to this rule was if a prisoner agreed to join the winning side after being defeated, but this was limited to foot soldiers. For officers, most of the time, they were executed if captured, unless they escaped before losing a battle.

In addition, one must consider the fact that by 1916, Villa was being vigorously pursued by two superior armies; the army under General Obregón, and the well-equipped U.S. Calvary of General Pershing. General Obregón had orders to take whatever action was necessary to capture or execute Villa. General Pershing had explicit military orders to capture Villa, dead or alive.

Other atrocities attributed to Villa involved the treatment accorded the Spaniards and Chinese. Villa hated the Spaniards because he was convinced that they had gained their wealth from the Mexican people who were held in peonage and serfdom for hundreds of years. When he confiscated their property, he did not hesitate to redress the injustices that occurred since days of Hernan Cortes. He believed there was no need for legal deliberations to redistribute their wealth to the Mexican people. Moreover, Villa needed the proceeds from the haciendas and the well-to-do to sustain the Division del Norte with military pay, food, munitions, and the trains he needed to deploy his army.

Villa hated the Chinese because at one time they tried to poison his soldiers, and he swore he would seek revenge against them for their act of betrayal. The fear by the Chinese was such that in February 1917, when General Pershing's column departed from Mexico, it included 500 Chinese nationals. For the Chinese to receive safe passage to enter the U.S., they were given an exemption from the Chinese Exclusionary Law.

Pancho Villa's Lifestyle

As a young man, Villa suffered many injustices, and he never enjoyed a family life. Beginning at age sixteen; he spent the next sixteen years in the mountains avoiding capture by the dreaded Rurales under the policies of Dictator Porfirio Diaz. At age thirty-two, he joined the Revolution to fight President Diaz, Pascual Orozco, Victoriano Huerta, and Carranza for the next ten years. By the time he received amnesty at age forty-two, he only managed to live three more years as a free man at his hacienda El Canutillo. Contrary to what some of his critics believe, Villa did not smoke or drink alcohol (except on special occasions). He had very bad teeth because he loved to eat candy. He loved to dance, had a decent voice for singing, and could also play the guitar. He loved children, and more than any other leader of the Revolution, he did his best to raise funds for the widows and orphans of the Revolution.

Throughout the Revolution, Villa rode many mounts and each time he would name his horse "Siete Leguas" (seven leagues), presumably because a good horse could gallop about 21 miles per day (one league is equal to three miles). He would change horses often because his mounts would get worn out or get injured in battle. Villa was an excellent rider and always instructed his men to take good care of their horses. During battle, it was his trademark to ride at full gallop at the head of a cavalry charge. He understood the value of horses so well that he was the first general of the Revolution since the Civil War to establish an elite cavalry, Los Dorados de Villa, a cavalry group of about 200 men who were handpicked by Villa for their horsemanship, bravery, and marksmanship. Los Dorados de Villa were regularly called upon to lead cavalry charges against the enemy to break their will to fight.

Guerilla Warfare Tactics

The Hat Trick

The Hat Trick was the first trick employed by Pancho Villa in 1911. When ordered to attack the City of Chihuahua, he was aware the Federales of President Diaz would be arriving as reinforcements by train. On the outskirts of Chihuahua City, the train needed to climb a steep grade. As the train chugged up the grade, a few Villa troops placed their hats on top of large rocks and fired a few shots at the train. This caused the Federales to immediately begin firing at the hats. The mass of Villa's troops were actually deployed further along the railroad line and as the train reached the top of grade, Villa's troops opened up with concentrated fire. Villa was not able to gain a complete victory because the Federales had machine guns and their trained military commander was quick to order a counter-attack. The Hat Trick was an important tactic for Villa for three reasons. He learned how to apply guerilla tactics under battle conditions, he learned that the Federales were better trained in military tactics than his troops, and he learned that he should always plan for a counter-attack.

Sagebrush

During the first part of the Revolution, when his army was small, Villa used sagebrush to fool the enemy. He would order a few men with their mounts to drag sagebrush back and forth, near the enemy camp. As the cloud of dust became visible, it fooled the enemy into believing that Villa had a large army. This would put fear into the enemy and when Villa attacked, the enemy actually believed they were being attacked by a superior force.

The Mexican Flag

In 1916, Villa came very close to being captured while being pursued by the troops of General Pershing. In March 1916, Col. Dodd, U.S. Army, had intelligence reports that Villa was hiding in the small village of Guerrero, Chihuahua. Col. Dodd ordered a forced march of his cavalry to ambush Villa where he would employ a traditional, high powered cavalry charge. When he arrived at Guerrero he ordered a halt because he saw a column of soldiers leaving the village with the Mexican Flag openly displayed. At first Col. Dodd believed the column of soldiers belonged to the Mexican Army under Carranza. When Col. Dodd realized the column were Villistas, he ordered a re-start of the cavalry charge. However, by now the Villistas were too far away to be captured. The surprise attack at Guerrero was the closest the U.S. Army came to capturing Villa during the Punitive Expedition.

The Trojan Horse

In 1914, Villa was ordered to capture Ciudad Juarez, along the U.S.-Mexican border. Ciudad Juarez was an important military target because the city was a port of entry for munitions from the U.S., and it was a large city with ample supply of monies, horses, and supplies. At first, Villa was not able to capture Juarez because his army was not strong enough and had to retreat to Chihuahua City. At Chihuahua City he got an idea on how he could capture Juarez. His plan was to capture the coal fueling station 100 miles from Juarez. At the coal fueling station, he ordered the Telegrapher to send a message to the army commander in Juarez saying that Villa had plans to capture an incoming coal train, and what was the Telegrapher to do? The army commander told the Telegrapher to order the train conductor to immediately return the train to Juarez. On the way to Juarez, Villa would resend the message about the Villistas trying to capture the coal train, and each time he they were told to bring the train in without any delay. In the meantime, at the coal fueling station, Villa had loaded the train with 1,500 cavalry troops. The Villistas arrived at Juarez at 5 AM, and proceeded to the center of the city. The Villistas dismounted and captured the city and 7,000 Federal troops without firing a shot. For this fete, the American generals along the Mexican border were amazed as how Villa was able to pull this Trojan Horse trick without having been trained in military tactics.

Chapter XVIII. Mercenaries

American

Throughout the Revolution, over 100 foreign mercenaries served in the armies of Villa, Carranza, and Zapata. Supposedly, they served for "gold and glory." The majority were U. S. citizens, who had gained experience in the Indian Wars, Spanish-American War, and the Filipino Rebellion. Americans in the Revolution included Oscar Creighton, an expert with dynamite; Tom Mix, a Texas Cowboy, who had served with the U.S. Army, and after leaving the Revolution went on to make several cowboy silent movies in Hollywood; Edwin "Tex" O'Reilly; and Thomas Fountain, a machine gunner who served with Villa and was executed by Pascual Orozco near Parral, Chihuahua. One of the most colorful adventurers was Ambrose Bierce, a noted Civil War author, who travelled to Mexico to join the Revolution, but disappeared after visiting the battlefield in Ciudad Juarez in 1913, Emil Holmdahl, served with Madero and Villa, and as a Scout with the Gen. Pershing's Punitive Expedition. In 1926, he was arrested in Parral, Chihuahua for stealing Pancho Villa' head from the local cemetery. He was released because the charges could not be proven.

Gregorio Cortez

After being released from an American prison, Gregorio Cortez crossed the border to fight in the Mexican Revolution.

Gregorio Cortez was a small farmer who grew corn near Austin, Texas. On June 12, 1901, he was visited by Karnes County Sheriff W. T. Morris, who accused him and his brother, Romaldo, of stealing a horse. Sheriff Morris spoke English, and the Cortez brothers spoke mostly Spanish. Morris asked if they had recently acquired a horse a "caballo" or a stallion. Gregorio answered he had acquired a "yegua," a mare. Since there was a language difference, an argument ensued. Morris shot and wounded Romaldo, and Gregorio shot and killed Morris. Gregorio and his brother escaped to a nearby ranch owned by Mr. Schnabel where they were found by a posse headed by Sheriff Glover. Shots were exchanged, and Gregorio killed Glover and Schnabel. Gregorio then escaped again and walked 100 miles to a ranch of a friend, Ceferino Flores, who gave him a horse, so he could escape to Laredo, Texas.

Gregorio was a fugitive for 12 days but captured when he was betrayed by a friend. The manhunt for Gregorio involved hundreds of men who had formed up from all over Texas to catch Gregorio. Many Anglos wanted swift justice, while many Mexican-Americans considered his effort to escape to be heroic.

At one time a vigilante group of 300 tried to hang him before he had been convicted of a crime. Gregorio had evaded capture by riding horses for 400 miles and running for 100 miles, though in the end, he was sentenced to 50 years in prison. In 1913, he was released from prison when he was pardoned by Governor Oscar Colquitt. Soon after his release, he crossed the border to join the Mexican Revolution. He soon tired of the Revolution and returned to the U.S., where he died on February 28, 1916, of pneumonia.

Other Foreign Soldiers

Foreign mercenaries included Col. Maximilian Kloss from the German Army who served with Gen. Alvaro Obregon and commanded his artillery during the Battle for Celaya; Giuseppi Garibaldi, the grandson of the Italian patriot who served with Madero in the first part of the Revolution; Lou Carpientier, an artillery officer from France, Benjamin Viljeon, a veteran from the

Boer War; Captain Ivor Thord-Gray from Switzerland; and A. W. Lewis, from Canada.

Chapter XIX. The Demise of the Personalities

Candido Aguilar

Aguilar was the Secretary of Foreign Affairs in the Carranza cabinet. He served as confidential ambassador on various assignments. He went into exile in the United States following the murder of President Carranza in 1920. He returned to Mexico to support the 1923-1924 de la Huerta uprising against Obregón, and went into exile again when the revolt failed. He received amnesty by President Lázaro Cárdenas and returned to Mexico 1939; elected deputy and then senator from Veracruz to the Congress; awarded the Legion of Honor by President Alemán in 1949. He died March 20, 1960, in Mexico City, DF.

Newton Baker

Secretary of War Newton Baker resigned as Secretary of War in 1921. He returned to the practice of law with Baker & Hostetler. The law firm he founded is one of the nation's 100 largest firms. Baker died on December 25, 1937 at age 66 in Shaker Heights, Ohio.

Luz Corral

After the death of Villa, she spent the rest of her life at Quinto Sol, a large estate built for her in Chihuahua City. Quinto Sol became a famous museum where tourists from all over the world could learn the story of the legendary Pancho Villa. Luz Corral, the only legal wife of Pancho Villa died in 1981.

James Creelman

A reporter during the height of yellow journalism, he could not stay away from writing, and returned to the World Journal to cover World War I for Hearst. On his way to the front to cover the war, Creelman died suddenly in Berlin of Bright's disease.

Felix Díaz (nephew of President Porfirio Díaz)

After Madero's arrest, Díaz signed the Embassy Pact (Pacto de la Embajada), facilitated by American Ambassador Henry Lane Wilson, which allowed General Huerta to become President. The understanding was that Díaz would run as presidential candidate the next election. Huerta did not honor the agreement and sent Díaz to Japan as an ambassador. After his return Díaz, was constantly harassed by Huerta, causing him to go into exile to New York and later Havana. He returned to Mexico in May 1916 and became the leader of the National Reorganizer Army (Ejército Reorganizador Nacional). His new revolutionary effort failed and was forced to retreat to the south of Mexico. In 1920, Díaz went into exile again, and returned in 1937 to settle in the City of Veracruz, where he died in 1945.

Lindley Garrison

Garrison served as Secretary of War from 1913 to 1916. Garrison and President Wilson never fit well together. Garrison urged American intervention in the Mexican revolution to restore order. Garrison supported a plan for expanding the U.S. military with what he called the Continental Army Plan. Garrison's proposal would establish a standing army of 140,000 and a national, volunteer reserve force of 400,000 men. After leaving Wilson's Administration, Garrison returned to the practice of law in the firm of Hornblower, Miller & Garrison. He died in Sea Bright, New Jersey in 1932.

General Pablo Gonzalez

During the interim presidency of Adolfo de la Huerta, Gonzalez was arrested when he was accused of treason and sedition. Initially he was sentenced to be executed, but was pardoned and instead went into exile in the U.S. After General Obregon's victory over Carranza, he returned to Mexico. Gonzalez retired from active duty and politics and went into the banking business. He was left almost destitute by the collapse of his bank and died in 1950 in the City of Monterrey.

Genovevo Rivas Guillén

Lt. Guillén, was the Mexican Army commander at the Carrizal, Chihuahua skirmish. He reported U.S. casualties were 50 soldiers killed, 27 prisoners captured, as well as horses and munitions. After the Battle of Carrizal, Lieutenant Rivas became Commander of Military Zone XIV, and fought during the Cristero War of 1926 in the states of Jalisco and San Luis Potosi. He became a Brigadier General in 1938, and became the military commander of the states of Queretaro, Oaxaca and Sonora. After retiring from the army, he devoted his time to agriculture. He drowned at Potrero de Para, San Luis Potosi, in 1947.

Eulalio Gutierrez

On July 2, 1915, Gutierrez formally resigned the Presidency he was accorded at the Aguascalientes Convention. He left for the United States and returned to Mexico in 1920 under amnesty by President Obregón, and was later elected as senator and governor of Coahuila in 1928. He publicly criticized the reelection of Álvaro Obregón and Plutarco Elías Calles. He joined the rebellion of José Gonzalo Escobar. After the Escobar rebellion failed, he went to live in San Antonio, Texas and did not return to Mexico until 1935. Four years later, he died in the City of Saltillo.

William Randolph Hearst

One of the most influential movie films of all time was Orson Welles' 1941 film "Citizen Kane," which was loosely based on parts of Hearst's life. Hearst used all his resources and influence in an unsuccessful attempt to prevent the film's release. Citizen Kane was twice ranked No.1 on the list of the American Film Institute's 100 greatest films of all time. Hearst's own image has largely been shaped by the film which paints a dark portrait of him. He died in Beverly Hills on August 14, 1951, at the age of 88.

Adolfo de la Huerta

De la Huerta started a failed revolt in 1923 against President Álvaro Obregón- whom he denounced as being corrupt. Obregón crushed the rebellion and forced De La Huerta into exile. On March 7, 1924, de la Huerta fled to Los Angeles and Obregón ordered the execution of every rebel officer with a rank higher than a major.

Jose Limantour

Towards the end of the Diaz government, Diaz felt that Limantour was becoming too powerful, and thus sent him to Europe to negotiate loans. Then, in 1911, after the collapse of the government, he returned to Mexico and encouraged Díaz to resign. They both went to live in France, where Limantour died in 1935.

John Lind

Following the assassination of Mexican President Francisco Madero in 1913, it became clear that U.S. Ambassador Henry Lane Wilson was complicit in the plot. As soon as the new U.S. President Woodrow Wilson and Secretary of State William Jennings Bryan assumed office on March 15, 1913, they sent John Lind to Mexico as Wilson's personal envoy for Mexican affairs. He died on September 18, 1930 at age 76 in Minneapolis, Minnesota.

General Hugh Scott

General Scott retired from the U.S. Army in May 1919. He served on the Board of Indian Commissioners from 1919 to 1929, and was the Chairman of the New Jersey State Highway Commission from 1923 to 1933. In 1928, he published an autobiography, "Some Memories of A Soldier." He died in Washington D.C. on April 30, 1934 at age 80.

Hipolito Villa

After Villa's death, Hipolito stayed on to administer El Canutillo ranch. He was a poor administrator and was eventually removed from the ranch. Years later, he faded into history and was able to live on a pension granted to him as a retired General. He died in 1964 in Chihuahua City.

Henry Lane Wilson

On July 17, 1913, President Wilson replaced him as Ambassador by sending his personal envoy John Lind, the former governor of Minnesota. During the First World War, Wilson served on the Commission for Relief in Belgium and in 1915, accepted the chairmanship of the Indiana State Chapter of the League to Enforce Peace, a position he held until his resignation over U.S. involvement in the League of Nations. Wilson published his memoir in 1927, and died in Indianapolis in 1932. He is buried in Crown Hill Cemetery, Indianapolis.

Chapter XX.   The Zimmerman Telegram

Theoretical Code used in the Zimmerman Telegram

[The following theoretical Number Code refers to the author's inferences of potential messages.]

Code	Meaning	Code	Meaning
1610	offer to	2010	authorized
1900	and	2040	against
1920	declares	3010	mexico
1930	war	3050	repossess
1940	make	5010	arizona
1950	to	5020	new mexico
1960	if	5040	united states

Message

2010 1950 1940 1610 3010 1960 3010. 1960 3010
1920 1930 2040 5040, 2010 1950 3050 5010 1900
5020.

Meaning

Authorized to make offer to Mexico. If Mexico
declares war against the United States,
authorized to repossess Arizona and New
Mexico.

In January 1917, the British Government code breakers intercepted a secret message sent from Berlin by German Foreign Minister von Eckhardt to Arthur Zimmerman, the German Minister in Mexico. The telegram contained secret information offering Mexico the return of Arizona, New Mexico, and Texas, if it would declare war against the United States.

Some historians have offered the explanation that the Zimmerman Memorandum was the main reason for ordering the return of the Punitive Expedition sent to Mexico to capture Pancho Villa. They believed it was necessary for Pershing to return the U.S. to start preparing for WW I. Although the reasoning sounds plausible, it is not supported for several reasons:

- The Zimmerman Telegram was intercepted in January 1917, but was not presented to the U.S. until February 24, 1917. By February 24, 1917, the Punitive Expedition had been withdrawn from Mexico when it re-entered the U.S. in January 1917. The U.S. did not declare war on Germany until April 6, 1917, and did not enter into combat operations until October 23, 1917.

- There is no evidence that Mexico seriously considered the German offer. There were no economic or military advantages for Mexico to go war with the U.S. to support the war effort of a European nation.

- Mexico did not have the arms and munitions to fight the U.S., and Germany was geographically too distant from Mexico to provide the armaments and munitions necessary to sustain a prolonged war effort. Conversely, the Carranza government was wholly dependent on U.S. arms to fight the Revolution taking place in Mexico. Had Carranza declared war against the U.S., the Mexican armies would have been crushed along the same lines as in the war of 1846-48 between the U.S. and Mexico.

- Mexico would not want to go to war with the U.S. because it would lose a great deal if it was defeated, once again, by the U.S. (as in the Texas revolt of 1836, annexation of Texas in 1845, and the war with Mexico in 1846-48.

- Moreover, the German offer to return land ceded by Mexico to the United States in 1846-48, did not include the return of California, which was the prize territory that the U.S. coveted when it went to war with Mexico in 1846-48.

The failure by General Pershing to capture Pancho Villa is the main reason the U.S. ordered the return of the Punitive Expedition. Initially, General Pershing believed he could overwhelm Mexico with 10,000 troops and easily capture Pancho Villa. When General Pershing was unable to capture Pancho Villa, the U.S. had to face certain realities:

- General Pershing failed to achieve his military objective of capturing Pancho Villa. Instead of capturing Pancho Villa, General Pershing entered into military engagements at Parral and Carrizal, Chihuahua, with Carranza troops, rather than Pancho Villa.

- The deployment of over 10,000 troops into the interior of Mexico, a sovereign nation, was an act of war that could not be justified.

- The U.S. Army troops sent to Mexico were sent in an arbitrary and capricious manner because it was done unilaterally without the consent or approval of Primer Jefe Carranza.

- President Wilson believed that the presence of the U.S. Army in Mexico would be welcomed. On the contrary, the U.S. Army in Mexico was met with resistance and hostility. Equally important, the 500 mile penetration by General Pershing left him vulnerable to guerilla attack on his supply lines from the rear. Also, the cost of maintaining a 10,000 man army was becoming prohibitive, which would eventually create a backlash with the American public.

After the firefight in Carrizal in June of 1916, the U.S. Army laid dormant at Colonia Dublan, near Columbus, New Mexico. Thus, after May 1916, the U.S. Army served no purpose in Mexico, except that it needed more time in Mexico to initiate an honorable withdrawal. The Punitive Expedition left Mexico because it failed to capture Pancho Villa. From a diplomatic point of view, the threat of German assistance, attributed to the Zimmerman telegram, was not a sustainable reason for leaving Mexico.

The real reason the U.S. entered WW I was the imminent threat of U-Boat attacks by Germany on U.S. shipping in the Atlantic Ocean. The proffered reason that the U.S. needed to withdraw General Pershing to get ready for WW I is misleading and only serves to cover up two central points: the U.S. failed in its military objective of capturing Pancho Villa and, after the Parral and Carrizal military engagements, the U.S. was on the brink of all-out war with Mexico.

Epilogue

The Revolution lasted ten years, and from this experience we learned two things: dictatorships that have been in place for many years are hard to remove, and the United States, due its geographical proximity, political and economic interests, will always be intertwined in the economic and internal affairs of Mexico.

Dictators are Difficult to Remove

The immediate objective of the Revolution of 1910, to remove President Diaz, was accomplished within six months. The Revolution started on November 20, 1910, and six months later, by May 1911, President Diaz had agreed to leave Mexico to live in Paris, France (Treaty of Ciudad Juarez). The departure of President Diaz did not end the Revolution because President-elect Francisco Madero was not sufficiently astute to take firm control of the internal affairs of Mexico. He failed to understand that he needed to be decisive in removing the entrenched powerbase left in place by Dictator Diaz. Even before he assumed the Presidency, he made several critical mistakes. His first mistake, according to the Plan of San Luis Potosi to start the revolution, Madero was to become the Provisional President as soon as President Diaz was removed. Instead of assuming the Presidency, as a concession to the Diaz regime, he agreed to designate Francisco de la Barra as acting Provisional President. Allowing De la Barra to become the leader of Mexico in effect prevented Madero from assuming full control of the government for six critical months, or until he was formally elected in November 1910. More importantly, during this period he allowed his detractors to entertain his demise. His second mistake was his agreement to retain the generals of the Mexican Army as the defenders of the country. This was another ill-conceived concession because these were the same generals that were indoctrinated by President Diaz to uphold the tactics of a dictatorship. Madero made the false assumption that the generals of the Diaz regime would be loyal to a new democratic form of government. As matters turned out, within thirteen months of assuming the Presidency, President Madero and Vice President Pino Suárez were assassinated by orders of General Victoriano Huerta. President Madero had placed his trust in General Huerta, whom he had unwittingly entrusted to defend him during the revolt against his Presidency (Ten Tragic Days).

As soon as General Huerta assumed the Presidency, Venustiano Carranza, the opportunist, declared he was now Primer Jefe of Mexico. Carranza cleverly chose the small hacienda by the name of Guadalupe, in his home State of Coahuila, to formulate his manifesto against General Huerta. Carranza was well aware that his manifesto would not be contested because the leaders of the Revolution, at this juncture, were more focused on removing General Huerta for his betrayal than paying attention to the implications inherent the Plan de Guadalupe. Thus, when Carranza seized the opportunity to become the leader of Mexico, his motives appeared to be lofty, but his real intent was to become the President of Mexico by whatever means were necessary.

The actions of Carranza during the military campaign to remove General Huerta clearly demonstrated he was willing to destroy Pancho Villa, so he could become the President of Mexico. To bring about the demise of Pancho Villa, Carranza developed a negative propaganda campaign to malign his reputation. He paid Mexican and American lobbyists to write negative newspaper and magazines articles in Mexico and the U.S. stating that Villa was an ordinary bandit and not fit to be a general of the Revolution. He also took action to prevent Villa from becoming the first General of the Revolution to reach Mexico City when he ordered Villa to loan his best troops to General Panifilo Natera to attack the City of Saltillo; he denied Villa the coal needed for his military trains to attack the City of Zacatecas, and he attempted to coerce Villa to resign as the General of the Division del Norte. Lastly, he contravened the outcome of the Aguascalientes Convention when he refused to vacate the position of Primer Jefe, even though the majority had voted him out and had elected Eulalio Gutierrez as the Provisional President.

That Carranza would die by assassination was quite predictable. In the end, Carranza died by assassination in 1920, when his most loyal supporter, General Alvaro Obregón, turned against him. No doubt, those that sought to eliminate Carranza could not overlook the deaths of two icons of the Revolution eliminated by Carranza: the assassination of Emiliano Zapata, and the execution of General Felipe Ángeles in 1919.

Protection of United States Investments

For many years, capitalists from the U.S. and Europe invested heavily in Mexico, at the invitation of the dictator President Diaz, to the detriment of his own people (Los Cientificos). As a result, foreigners owned or controlled substantial interests in land, cattle, mineral mines, Mexico's railroad system, and its huge oil deposits. These vast holding were monitored by a cadre of U.S. Consulate Offices stationed throughout the major cities of Mexico, whose job was to protect American business interests and American profits. In addition, President Wilson also assigned two special envoys, George Carothers and Leon Canova, to maintain a one-on-one liaison with Carranza and Villa, respectively. President Wilson wanted to be constantly informed about the political inclinations and the military plans of Villa and Carranza.

Covert action by U.S. Ambassador Henry Lane Wilson

When the Revolution started in 1910, the U.S. was taken by surprise on how quickly the nation marched against the dictatorship of President Diaz. As soon as Madero assumed the Presidency, the U.S. immediately sought to protect American interests by economic, political, or military means.

The first to take action against the interests of Mexico was U.S. Ambassador Henry Lane Wilson. As soon as Madero assumed the Presidency, Ambassador Wilson embarked on a determined campaign to ensure the downfall of President Madero when he plotted with a number of Mexican generals to overthrow the Madero Presidency. The historical evidence available makes it clear that the Mexican generals would not have plotted or succeeded in their plan to overthrow President Madero without the direct involvement and political support of Ambassador Wilson. When President Madero was elected, the U.S. stood at the crossroads of supporting democracy for Mexico, and thus set an example for all of Latin American countries. Instead of ensuring that democracy would flourish, the U.S. conspired to bring about the death of the first democratically elected president in Mexico since the thirty-year reign of President Porfirio Diaz.

President Wilson: Intervention and Occupation

As soon as President Madero was betrayed by General Victoriano Huerta, the U.S. moved decisively to control the internal affairs of Mexico. In 1913, President Wilson stated that General Huerta would be removed "by force if necessary." In 1914, President Wilson ordered the U.S. Atlantic Fleet to the Port of Tampico, as well as the military occupation of the Port of Veracruz. In 1915, at Agua Prieta, Sonora, he engineered the destruction of Pancho Villa's Army by providing U.S. Army military trains for the Army of Carranza, and in 1916, he ordered the capture of Pancho Villa by decapitation for raiding the small village of Columbus, New Mexico.

When General Huerta assumed the Presidency it was not necessary for President Wilson to intervene in the internal affairs of Mexico. General Huerta was going to be removed because of the callous and treacherous manner in which he had betrayed President Madero and the nation. After General Huerta committed his coup d'état, he was opposed by the military forces of Pancho Villa, Emiliano Zapata, Venustiano Carranza, Pablo Gonzalez, and Alvaro Obregón. The new leaders of the Revolution constituted a powerful military force determined to remove Huerta. The Revolutionaries had been united in defeating the Mexican Army of the Dictator Diaz, the insurrection of Pascual Orozco, and they now were more galvanized than ever to remove General Huerta. The combined forces of the Revolutionaries totaled over 60,000 troops, almost four times as many as was needed to defeat President Diaz. In addition, by the time the U.S. decided to occupy the Port of Veracruz, Pancho Villa was already on the march with the most powerful army of the Revolution. His army, including an elite mobile cavalry, was poised to take the strategic cities of Ciudad Juarez, Chihuahua City, Saltillo, Torreon, and Zacatecas. When Pancho Villa defeated the Federales in the City of Zacatecas, without any help from the U.S., victory was assured because President Huerta had lost the last fortified city on the road to Mexico City. It was only a matter of time before

General Huerta would surrender, which he did in June 1914.

The demand by Admiral Mayo, for the Mexican Navy to fly the American flag and render a 21-naval gun salute, was a clear act of arrogance towards Mexico. Moreover, only a few days after the demand for a 21-gun salute was made, the U.S. Navy ordered several battleships to pulverize the Port of Veracruz. For this action, the U.S. awarded the Medal of Honor commendation to 52 sailors and marines for valor during combat, when in fact the U.S. battleships had already destroyed the defenseless Mexican Navy. The occupation of the Port of Veracruz was an unjustifiable act of war, and when the Mexican Navy fought back, President Wilson found it necessary to order the U.S. War College to prepare war plans in case Mexico declared war against the U.S.

Intercepting the German ship *Ypiranga* to prevent the delivery of arms to General Huerta was a violation of Mexico's sovereign rights as a nation to maintain an open port of entry. To stop the shipment of arms and munitions from reaching Mexico, according to international protocols, the U.S. Navy should have intercepted the *Ypiranga* on the high seas, not while the ship was anchored in the Port of Veracruz.

The action of President Wilson in authorizing the movement of 5,000 Carranza troops in 1915, from Eagle Pass, Texas, to Douglas, Arizona, on American railways and American soil, was an act of war and a violation of the U.S. Neutrality Laws. Without a doubt, the plan to transport Carranza troops was conceived by the American military, approved by President Wilson, and handed to Carranza as a gift to destroy Pancho Villa. This transporting of Carranza troops represents the largest mass movement of a foreign army on U.S. soil designed to impact the outcome of a battle in which the U.S. was not at war.

The Punitive Expedition of 1916 constituted an act of war against Mexico. By penetrating deep into the interior of Mexico with over 10,000 cavalry troops with the stated purpose of capturing Pancho Villa, the U.S. committed an act of war. Clearly, it was the intent of President Wilson to use the Punitive Expedition to destroy Pancho Villa once and for all. General Pershing's expedition failed to capture Pancho Villa for several reasons; Primer Jefe Carranza never supported the American intrusion into Mexico, Pancho Villa had the support of the Mexican people, and he knew that if he was captured, U.S. expansionists and war mongers would demand more territory from Mexico.

Unwarranted Deaths of American and Mexican Soldiers

The deaths of 27, and the capture of 24 American soldiers, as well as the death of 255 Mexican soldiers rest squarely on the shoulders of President Wilson as the Commander in Chief of the United States. None of the intrusions and interventions authorized by President Wilson were necessary to stabilize the internal matters of Mexico. The fact that the outcome of the Revolution did not unfold according to his personal expectations, was not justification for the military actions taken by President Wilson. In the final analysis, at the most crucial point in the Revolution when General Huerta betrayed President Madero, the leaders of the Revolution had sufficient military forces to remove General Huerta. Mexico did not need assistance from President Wilson to remove General Huerta. His fate was sealed when he betrayed President Madero and thus betrayed the Mexican people.

The Punitive Expedition only came about because President

Wilson authorized the use of military trains to defeat Villa at Agua Prieta. This caused Pancho Villa to seek retribution by attacking Columbus, New Mexico.

In retrospect, one can reasonably conclude that it was not necessary to send a "Punitive Expedition" of 10,000 cavalry troops into Mexico to catch one so-called bandit. The folly of the expedition became apparent, when after one year of operations in Mexico, the expedition returned to the U.S. empty handed, without ever capturing or even catching sight of Pancho Villa.

Misguided Intentions

Although President Wilson took aggressive action to change the outcome of the Revolution, he did not achieve the results he expected.

- The demand for the Mexican Navy to provide the U.S. Navy a 21- gun salute at Tampico was never delivered by the government of Victoriano Huerta.

- The interception of the German ship *Ypiranga* to stop munitions from being delivered to Victoriano Huerta failed. Days later, the *Ypiranga* moved to the nearby port of Nuevo Mexico and proceeded to unload the munitions.

- The naval blockade of the Port of Veracruz to intimidate Victoriano Huerta into resigning his Presidency failed. Huerta was removed from the Presidency by the armies of Zapata, Villa, Carranza, Obregon, and Gonzalez.

- The military effort in 1916 to transport Carranza troops on U.S. Army trains to ensure the collapse of Villa's Army at Agua Prieta failed to destroy Villa. For the next four years, Villa continued to field a formidable army against Carranza, until Villa retired from the Revolution.

- The Punitive Expedition ordered by President Wilson to capture Villa failed. After one year in Mexico, General Pershing returned to the U.S. without ever sighting or capturing Villa.

Pancho Villa into History

Pancho Villa was the most celebrated persona of the Mexican Revolution of 1910. One cannot speak of the Revolution without mentioning Pancho Villa, and one cannot speak of the Pancho Villa without mentioning the Revolution. He rose from the ashes of peonage to lead an army as large as 50,000 to remove the dictators Porfirio Diaz and Victoriano Huerta, and General Pascual Orozco. He fought Venustiano Carranza for six years to prevent him from becoming another dictator. He cemented his reputation as the greatest guerrilla fighter when he avoided capture by the American Army.

Evading capture by General Pershing is perhaps Villas' greatest legacy. Had Villa been captured, the Revolution would have resulted in a totally different outcome.

Pancho Villa died at age 45. He lived a harrowing experience, always on the cusp of death. As a cattle rustler from age 16 to 32 in the mountains of Chihuahua and Durango, he was almost killed several times when being pursued by the infamous Rurales. As a leader of the Revolution, he also was almost killed another several times: in 1911, when he mounted a hand grenade assault to defeat the Federal Army in Ciudad Juarez; when General Huerta ordered that he be executed before a firing squad for insubordination; an assassination plan ordered by Carranza; a plan by the Japanese to poison him; a military plan by President Wilson to destroy him in the battle for the City of Agua Prieta; a decapitation plan carried out by General Pershing to eliminate him; and when he almost died of a severe leg infection when shot by one of his own men while evading General Pershing.

Assassination was Inevitable

Because Pancho Villa had so many enemies during the Revolution, it was not unexpected he would be assassinated only three years after he retired. The world will never know if he was assassinated because he was threat to the new regime in Mexico or because someone sought revenge for past deeds. Throughout the Revolution, Pancho Villa was well aware that he was the subject of many assassination attempts. During his military campaigns, he would have his soldiers eat his food first to find out if it was poisoned. In the evenings he would go to sleep in one location and return the next day from a different direction.

When he received amnesty from the Mexican Government in 1920, he negotiated a requirement to be provided 50 of his beloved Dorados as personal escorts for protection. His escorts and his followers lived comfortably with him at the Hacienda El Canutillo, a hacienda that was granted to him by the terms of the amnesty. He prospered as gentleman rancher who introduced several modern farming practices. He lived happily with his latest wife Austerberta Renteria, and he was able to bring many of his offspring to live with him at El Canutillo. Unfortunately, on July 20, 1923, as he was leaving the City of Parral, he was assassinated in an ambush that was carefully planned by his adversaries. He died the way he lived, with a pistol in his hand, ready to engage the enemy, but it was too late. He died instantly when his body was riddled with eight bullets.

Legacy of Pancho Villa

In Part One of this book, European and United States Dominance, the authors cited the following passage by General John Eisenhower, "Poor Mexico, so far from God, and so close to the United States". The implication being that Mexico had a twofold problem: the Catholic Church would constantly dominate the religious development of Mexico's indigenous people, and Mexico would also be subject to the territorial ambitions of the United States.

Based on recent historical events, the authors believe that Mexico's twofold problem has now been largely resolved.

Since the days of the missions along El Camino Real and the War of the Cristeros, the Catholic Church in Mexico has been secularized. Although the Church continues to be the dominant religion, there is, nonetheless, freedom of religion, and there is a clear separation between the powers of the church and Mexico's fundamental form of government.

Regarding the ambition of the United States for additional Mexican territory, we believe that notion came to an end as a result the Mexican Revolution. The failure by the U.S. Army to capture Pancho Villa is the main reason the U.S. will no longer pursue territorial gains.

In the history of Mexico, two people stand above all others as protectors of the nation. Father Hidalgo gave birth to a new nation when he adopted the Virgin de Guadalupe as a flag for the independence of Mexico. He sacrificed his life to ensure that Mexico was for Mexicans and should not be subjugated by a foreign country. President Benito Juarez, a humble Indian from the State of Oaxaca, placed his life in danger when he declared that the monarchy of Maximilian would not be tolerated in Mexico. When all others believed that Mexico was doomed by foreign occupation, President Juarez fought the French Army until the monarchy of Maximilian was removed from Mexico.

General Francisco "Pancho" Villa also stands as another protector of the nation. Villa remained in the Revolution for ten years. He fought against the armies of President Diaz, the revolt of Pascual Orozco, the betrayal by General Victorian Huerta, against the dictatorship of Venustiano Carranza, and military aggression by President Wilson. If Villa had not been a true patriot, he could have quit the Revolution and left Mexico as a rich man. Having been brought into the Revolution by the patriotic beliefs of President Madero and Governor Abraham Gonzalez, Villa never contemplated leaving the Revolution. He never vacillated, and instead, he fought for the underdog and the nation when Mexico was invaded by the U.S. Army. Against an overwhelming military force, Villa avoided capture, and in doing so, he forced the U.S. Army to retreat from Mexico. Had Villa been captured, Mexico would have been disgraced as was the case when General Santa Anna was captured and he ceded the territory of Texas to the New Republic of Texas. Moreover, had Pancho Villa been captured, there is every reason to believe that Mexico could have lost the five northern states of Sonora, Chihuahua, Coahuila, Nuevo Leon, and Tamaulipas. At this crucial point in history, the U.S. had a large army in Mexico, war plans had been made to invade Mexico, and there existed a group of powerful expansionists with huge investments in Mexico.

By evading capture and forcing General Pershing to withdraw, Villa brought respect and dignity to the people of Mexico. Villa was able to overcome a defamation campaign by Primer Jefe Carranza to destroy his character, and when President

Wilson authorized military trains to transport troops intent on destroying his army at Agua Prieta, he retaliated by attacking Columbus, New Mexico. In spite of his faults, when Villa retired from the Revolution, he was given amnesty for his past indiscretions, a 25,000 acre ranch, and 50 of his Dorados de Villa as his personal escorts.

Upon closer examination of Carranza's role in the Revolution and President Wilson's arrogance in trying to annihilate Villa, one would have to conclude that Villa has not been accorded proper recognition for perseverance and resiliency as a protector of Mexico, and as the foremost warrior of the Revolution.

The authors of this book have taken a great deal of pleasure in investigating the complex life of Pancho Villa. We are absolutely sure this will not be the last book written on the life of Pancho Villa. His life will continue to be worthy of additional investigation.

According to General Hugh Scott, "If things were reversed, we would not allow any foreign country to be sloshing around in our country…miles from the border, no matter who they were."

Actual Military Incursion by General Pershing

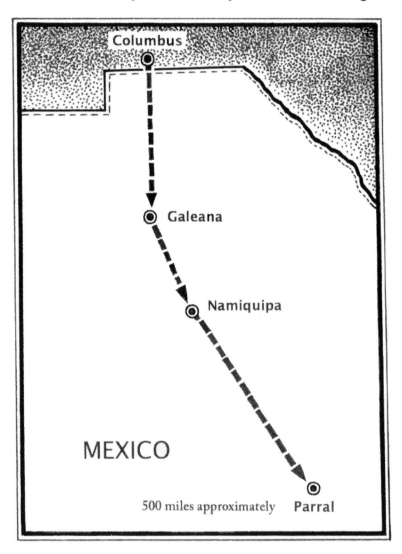

Theoretical Military Incursion by the Mexican Army

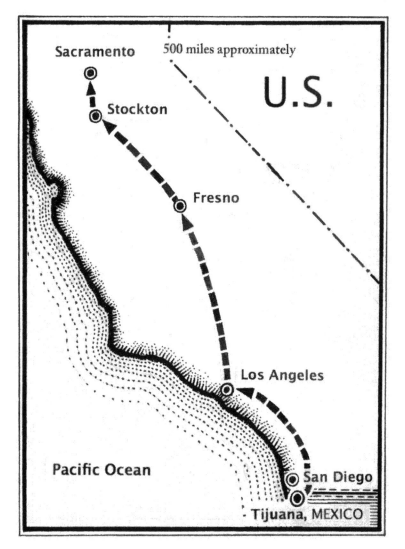

List of Maps

Bibliography

Mexican Government Publication, :Asi Fue La Revolución, Secretaria de Educación Publica, (1) Crisis del Porfirismo, (2) Caída de Antiguo Régimen, (3) Madero y El Tiempo Nuevo, 1986".

Braddy, Haldeen, Pancho Villa Rides Again, 1967. Paisano Press, El Paso, Texas.

Brenner, Anita, "The Wind That Swept Mexico," 1971. University of Texas Press, Austin, Texas.

Clendenen, Clarence, "The United States and Pancho Villa," A Study in Unconventional Diplomacy,

Cole, Merl Burke, Romantic Tragedies of Mexico, 1956, The Christopher Publishing House, Boston U.S.A.

Cumberland, C. C. "The Mexican Revolution, The Constitutionalist Years," 1972. University of Texas Press.

Davis, Burke, "Get Yamamoto," 1969. Random House, New York.

Guzman, Martin, "The Eagle and the Serpent". Peter Smith Publisher, 1969

Harris Irving, Clifford, 1982. "Tom Mix and Pancho Villa," New York, St. Martins Press.

Katz, F. "The Life and Times of Pancho Villa." Stanford University Press, 1998.

King, Rosa, E., "Tempest Over Mexico," 1935. Little, Brown, and Co. Boston

Lansford, William, "Pancho Villa," 1965. Los Ángeles, Shellbourne Press.

Machado, M. A. "Centaur of the North"; Francisco Villa, the Mexican Revolution and Northern Mexico. Arte Publico Press, 1996.

Metz, Leon, 1989. "Border — The U.S.-Mexico Line". El Paso, Texas, Mangan Books.

Millon, Robert, P., "Zapata," 1969. International Publishers, New York.

Osorio, Ruben, "The Secret Family of Pancho Villa," 2000. Center for Big Bend Studies, Alpine, Texas.

Pinchon, Edgecumb, "Viva Villa," 1933.

Plana, Manuel, "Pancho Villa and the Mexican Revolution". Interlink Books, 2002.

Quirk, R. E. "The Mexican Revolution," 1914-1915. Indiana University Press, 1960.

Reed, John, "Insurgent Mexico." Simon and Schuster, 1969.

Richmond, D. W. :Venustiano Carranza's Nationalist Struggle", 1983. University of Nebraska Press.

Ruiz, Ramon Eduardo, "The Great Rebellion," 1976. New York, Norton.

Womack, John, Jr., "Zapata and the Mexican Revolution," 1969. Alfred Knopf, New York.

Other Investigative Material

Cyrulik, John M. Major USA, "A Strategic Examination of the Punitive Expedition into Mexico," *1916-17,* 2003. Master of Military Art and Science, University of New York College, Brockport, N. Y.

Hyder, Victor D. Lt. Commander U.S. Navy, Decapitation Operations: Criteria for Targeting Enemy Leadership. U.S. Army Command and General Staff College, Fort Leavenworth, Kansas, 2004

Orr, Brent, Major NCARNG, "Borderline Failure: National Guard on the Mexican Border, 1916-1917", USA Command and Staff College, Fort Leavenworth, Kansas, AY 2011.

Pershing, John, Major General USA, Commanding General Punitive Expedition Report, U.S. Army Military History Institute, October 10, 1916

Sanchez Lamiego, Miguel (General Mexican Army), "La Invasion Espanola de 1829," (1971). Editorial JUS.MEXICO

Samuel S. Ortega was born in Santa María, California. He attended high school in Woodland, California, Sacramento City College and California State University, Sacramento. Ortega was also the recipient of a scholarship to attend the John F. Kennedy School of Government at Harvard University. He served as an Administrator in several agencies with the State of California. He was involved in  developing programs on job placement and unemployment insurance at the Employment Development Department, monitoring civil service hiring with the State Personnel Board, and monitoring minority and small business participation in highway construction with the Department of Transportation.

Ortega's parents were born in Dolores, Chihuahua and lived in Mexico during the Revolution, and not too far from many of Villa's battle areas and hideouts. During the turmoil they decided to move to the U. S. to seek a better life. According to Ortega's parents, they could cross the border into the U.S. by paying ten cents per person.

Concurrent with his state government experience, Ortega and his family have owned and operated several restaurants and night clubs in the Sacramento area. He is an avid reader on the Mexican Revolution and World War II. Ortega has conducted several diorama presentations at local schools and community organizations on the Mexican Revolution, the Battle of Midway, the Doolittle Raid, and the defense of Bastogne by the 101st Airborne Division, during WW II. Ortega served in the United States Army and was assigned to overseas duty in Germany.

Robert Hernandez was born in Sacramento, California. He attended high school at Zephyr Cove, Nevada, and furthered his education at Sacramento City College and California State University. While at Sacramento State, Robert was elected President of the Student Senate.  Robert was employed by the State Personnel Board to improve the hiring practices of the State of California; at the Department of Transportation, in programs relating to civil rights hiring, and Information Technology. Robert and his family have owned and operated several restaurants in Davis, California, named Casa Hernandez.

Robert has considerable experience in researching indigenous Mexican History and Archeology. He has travelled to Mexico to study Mesoamerican civilization, including an investigation of the codices related to the Mexica and Mayan civilizations and their language.

Robert's grandfather, who happened to be a very good marksman, fought with Pancho Villa's army as a cavalryman. Unwilling to be involved in the Revolution any longer, he left his home of Jalpa, Zacatecas, moved to Arizona, and later settled in the Salinas Valley. When he arrived in the U.S., he registered for the military draft at age 26. It should be noted that the City of Zacatecas was the scene of the bloodiest battles of the Revolution. The City of Zacatecas was continuously heavily reinforced by the Federales because its railroad system was the gateway to Mexico City.

Index